RETHINK IMPOSTER SYNDROME

Build confidence, beat self-doubt and succeed

VINITA BANSAL

CONTENTS

INTRODUCTION

HOW WOULD YOU define a life well lived?

A life of no regrets?

Life presents many scenarios where you need to choose between multiple options. Other than making the best decision in the moment, you can never know for sure which option will lead to a better outcome in the future. Even when the decision turns out well and brings success in one area of your life—let's say a successful career—you may regret being a failure in other aspects—say as a parent or a spouse.

Regret is the emotion we all experience when we're dissatisfied with our present situation and imagine a better future only if we had done something different in the past. Whether it's regretting the years you have wasted in your life not living up to your own expectations or the opportunities you let by that existed in the past but no longer exist and are lost forever, it's these choices—the ones you made and the ones you did not—that shape you into the person you're today. Living a life of no regrets will be living a life without its experiences—facing the ups and downs is what motivates us to avoid repeating mistakes. Instead of a thing to avoid, regret is a positive force in human life.

When feeling is for thinking and thinking is for doing, regret is for making us better — Daniel H. Pink[1]

A life full of happiness?

We all seek joy in our life and that's not a bad thing. The constant desire to improve ourselves and our life situation, seeking a better life, or the pursuit of pleasure is what keeps the human race thriving. It's chasing happiness that adds to our misery.

I'll be happy when I'll have a bigger house.
I'll be happy when I get into the college of my choice.
I'll be happy when I get a promotion.

Thinking this way sets us on a hedonic treadmill constantly chasing the next big target. We set goals and expectations—getting the next big promotion, completing a complex task, or finishing up a really big project. We run to gain those things, often working every waking hour and going to extremes to improve ourselves imagining all along the way how happy we would be when we achieve this goal. But once we succeed or reach that destination, instead of being euphoric, the feeling is more of a relief—getting closure on all the effort leading up to this moment. The happiness—if it does show up—is only momentary, often lasting a few hours, days, or sometimes even a week.

There's another problem with using happiness as a measure of a life well-lived. Trying to be happy all the time leaves no room for negative emotions. So, when they do show up, we instinctively treat them as harmful. But humans have been enlisted with negative emotions for a reason. They're a powerful motivator in our desire to lead a better life. We all deal with negativity from time to time simply because it's part of the human condition.

Happiness is the universal temperature reading of our emotional well-being. This is why we frequently ask ourselves whether we're happy. It's why people ask us if we're happy. But happiness is fleeting — Marshall Goldsmith[2]

A life free of financial insecurity?

A certain amount of financial freedom is essential to live a comfortable life—in which you don't feel poor and miserable. In that sense, money can buy you certain things—clothes, food, child care, home, cars, or anything else you may want or need. But the thing with money is that it's never enough. Once you reach your ultimate financial goal, you want more.

Money is necessary to a certain extent, but it can't change the way you think about yourself. It can't make you confident, free from self-doubt, or rid you of all your insecurities.

Make money the measure and you are in for trouble for that would keep you in its grip forever — B.S. Murthy[3]

A life with meaningful relationships?

Having friends and family who support you, who cheer for you, and who love you is a huge motivational factor in our lives. Meaningful social relationships not only increase our ability to cope with stress or adversity, but also play a crucial role in our ability to learn, grow, explore, achieve goals, cultivate new talents, and find purpose and meaning in life.[4] They strengthen our feelings of control and confidence thereby playing a vital role in our overall well-being.

Warmth, admiration, and respect from people close to us brings a sense of happiness, contentment, and calmness that makes us thrive. When we don't have strong relationships or the ones that bring out the worst in us, we feel anxious, depressed, and lonely. In that sense, meaningful relationships are an essential component of living a good life. But by themselves, they're not enough.

While relationships make us happy, they do not always bring satisfaction to our lives. Satisfaction comes with effort and sacrifice, from engaging in challenging and difficult situations, and from going after the things we find worthwhile. Real satisfaction doesn't come from getting what we want or living a comfortable life—they only bring momentary happiness—it comes from fully accepting our situation, experiencing the ups and downs as we go with the journey, and from trying, trying and trying. Lasting satisfaction comes from making progress towards something meaningful in our lives; it comes from growth.

To do what you wanna do, to leave a mark - in a way that you think is important and lasting - that's a life well-lived
— Laurene Powell Jobs

That's exactly the measure I wanted to have in my life. I didn't view a life well lived as a life of no regrets, filled with happiness and wealth, or having a huge supportive network—though those things are important in their own way—I wanted a life where I was brave enough to go after the things I desired. This in no way means living a fearless life or never doubting myself. I doubt myself plenty, I fear my decisions and I still worry that I won't be able to meet other people's expectations. Getting rid of self-doubt, insecurity, or fear of failure is not my goal because I have learned to live beside them without letting them get in my way.

Let me tell you a small story.

In the early years of my career, as a software developer, I traveled to work for a client in the US. I was leading the project to integrate our product into the client's production systems. It was a large organization and I was expected to coordinate and work with people who had years of experience. While waiting at the airport, every time my phone rang, I jumped from my seat—my boss must be calling to tell me that the plan has been canceled as I am not qualified for the job. Those feelings of inadequacy and self-doubt didn't end there. When I reached the client site, it was a new environment with a completely new experience. Each day I woke up with feelings of anxiety; every day I told myself a new self-defeating story:

They'll soon find out I know nothing.
How long before they know they made a wrong decision?
Oops, I made a mistake. It's all over!
Every aspect of my work has to be perfect or else they'll send me back.

Those thoughts and feelings that seemed so real at the time were all in my head. None of them turned out to be true. The project ended well and I got a promotion. More travel opportunities, more projects, and more customers landed my way. With each trip, every new project, and every customer, the same cycle of feeling inept, living with constant fear, and feeling relieved once it was all over repeated itself. That continued for years!

I switched jobs, got a new role with bigger and better opportunities. Getting ahead in my life should have made these feelings disappear—after all, I now had the skills that I didn't have earlier. But a step up in my role also stepped up my fears—with more to lose and so much at stake, those feelings of unworthiness and self-doubt got stronger and more intense. Between now and then, my self-doubt hasn't disappeared—it has stayed with me every step of the way. But one thing has changed. What earlier appeared as an impediment to my success, I later realized, is a side-effect of doing worthwhile work.

That self-doubt that once made me feel like a 'fake' now keeps me grounded and real. It makes me question my assumptions, challenges me to seek alternative opinions, and encourages me to keep looking when I haven't found a way. The fear of failure from doing something new still sits by my side, but that fear does not prevent me from going after the opportunities or the life I desire. The disappointment from making a mistake no longer leads to a downward spiral, it only ups my motivation to increase effort, try a different strategy, and work harder. Stepping outside my comfort zone earlier brought stress and anxiety, but not anymore. Adopting a learning attitude creates a sense of excitement which makes it easier for me to step into the unknown. Confidence, which I earlier thought I lacked, often using it as an excuse to quit trying, is now plenty. Bridging the confidence gap helped me see that confidence is not always a given, it's built along the way. And here's the best part. In my moments of struggle (which are a constant part of my life), I am no longer at the mercy of my thoughts. Learning to recalibrate my internal voice from being critical and judgmental to one that is forgiving and understanding has created a new way of life—one with the freedom and a sense of control to respond to life difficulties in a positive way; one in which I spend more time creating the life I want as opposed to feeling stuck or being a victim of my circumstances.

What about you? How do you deal with your own fears and insecurities? Do you recognize your unique talents or consider yourself unworthy of success? Do you accept positive feedback or shrug it aside with the view that others are wrong in crediting you? Do you embrace opportunities or let them go with the worry that any mistakes and failures will expose you? Do you go after the things you desire or keep putting them off for lack of confidence? Do you feel lonely in this experience?

Not being able to see the flaws in your thinking keeps you captive. Getting hooked by your thoughts and buying into your own self-defeating stories or responding to your limiting beliefs with mental shortcuts leads to serious thinking errors—you make terrible decisions with long-lasting effects. Cutting through that noise requires practicing good habits of the mind. It requires separating thoughts that push you forward from the ones that pull you down. It requires challenging stories that prevent you from seeing the true measure of your worth.

Consider the experience of journeying through a long, dark tunnel. You can either focus on the dark inside and feel constricted or you can slowly work your way through that lonely, dreary, dark tunnel in order to reach the other side. Journeying through that tunnel will be challenging. Navigating the discomfort won't be easy. But if you keep moving forward and doing your part, you'll eventually make it through. There will be moments when you're tempted to give up, when the work may seem too much, where irrespective of how much you try, you can't see the light at the end of the tunnel. Keeping your calm in those moments and thinking objectively can get you moving again. Ultimately, if you keep at it, you'll see the light at the end of the tunnel; what once seemed so distant will appear perfectly within your reach.

This book is that light at the end of the tunnel. By applying the practices in this book, you can re-emerge from the shadows of your thoughts into the lightness of your life.

HOW THIS BOOK WILL BENEFIT YOU

This book has all the tools and techniques that I have applied over the years. They will not turn you into a perfect human being who's free of self-doubt, anxiety, insecurity, or fear. That would be unrealistic given how our brain works. Rather, this book serves as a roadmap for real behavioral change, a new way of acting in which you manage your life according to your own values and what's important to you without feeling trapped by your most troubling thoughts. Feelings of unworthiness, lack of confidence, and the constant self-doubting that once appeared as obstacles in your life will now serve as a source of creativity, inspiration, and insight.

Instead of controlling your negative thoughts or forcing yourself to think positively—which usually doesn't work and can sometimes even be counterproductive—this book will enable you to connect even with your most troubling emotions thereby opening up the space between your feelings and how you respond to those feelings. Consciously choosing a response instead of being on autopilot will enable you to lead a life with intention instead of simply being carried along by the tide. If you're struggling to embrace the opportunities in your life or getting hooked by your thoughts and feelings is leading to self-sabotage behaviors (procrastination, perfectionism, people-pleasing), this book will show you how to navigate those emotions with courage and compassion so that they don't get in your way or prevent you from going after the big things in your life.

Aiming to be fearless or striving to be a certain way—with a certain amount of confidence, competence, or skills—will only set you up for disappointment, frustration, and failure. Rather, the book aims to let your fears sit by your side as you walk towards what matters to you. Tiny tweaks to your mindset, your beliefs, and your habits can bring a profound, lasting change in areas of life that matter to you.

With knowledge and research from neuroscience, philosophy, psychology, and many other fields, this book provides practical advice that's easy to understand and apply in real life. In *Rethink Imposter Syndrome*, you'll find these ten key ideas:

1. Embrace feelings of self-doubt, incompetence, and inadequacy to lead with courage and conviction.
2. Recognize your true worth by shining a light on your strengths and acknowledging your successes and skills.
3. Replace negative self-talk that highlights your insecurities with positive behaviors and attitudes.
4. Shift from comfort to stretch zone that ups your motivation to do better and fuels your productivity.
5. Let go of self-sabotage behaviors, perfectionism, and procrastination to reclaim your excellence.
6. Become more resilient by bouncing back from setbacks and feeling in control of your outcomes.
7. Discover the power of true confidence without faking your way through success.
8. Recalibrate your internal voice from being critical and judgmental to being kind and understanding.
9. Train your brain to repeat actions that will take you closer to your goals.
10. Bring lasting change by cultivating the right mindset to shape yourself into the person you wish to become.

Additionally, the book comes with 11 printable worksheets to help you:

- Determine the severity of your imposter feelings.

- Identify the root cause of your imposter syndrome to understand what feeds your inner critic.
- Apply the strategies in this book to real life with the help of guided exercises.
- Set goals that motivate you to become the best, most capable person you can be.

As you read the book, don't focus on what you're going to get. Focus on who you're becoming along the way. Small shifts in your behavior over time can transform your life by enhancing your ability to thrive. Your potential isn't limited. What you can achieve isn't limited. What's limiting are your beliefs. Don't let self-doubt hold you captive or stand in the way of your dreams. Believe in yourself, your abilities, and your potential because if you don't, then who will?

Part 1

Understanding Imposter Syndrome

CHAPTER 1

What Goes on in Your Head?

DO YOU OFTEN feel a wave of self-doubt coming on? Do you have a nagging feeling like you don't belong, you're not good enough, you don't deserve the promotion, or you aren't cut out to be in this position? What do you think about your achievements—do you believe it's a result of your skills and abilities or do you tend to attribute your success to luck, your ability to work harder than everyone else, knowing the right people, being in the right place at the right time, or simply your interpersonal charms like being funny, friendly or witty that makes you more likable?

You may not realize it, but you are equipped with great storytelling abilities. While you share a small part of these stories with people around you, a large and often invisible part of this storytelling goes inside your own head. Your inner dialogue governs not only your emotions but also plays a crucial role in determining how you act afterward.

Imagine this.

Your manager just announced an award for your exceptional performance. The award is to be handed over at the all-hands meeting next month in front of the entire organization. What's the first thought that comes to your mind? Would you feel a sense of accomplishment and congratulate yourself for doing so well or would you dread walking up the stage and being told that you are not worthy of this award and being exposed as a fraud?

In another instance, someone senior in the organization gives you positive feedback for handling a project well. Would you wholeheartedly accept the praise and feel worthy of this recognition or would you feel compelled to shrug it aside by telling them that you don't deserve this compliment "It was too easy. If I can do it, anyone can!" "I got lucky!" "It's not me. It's my team!"

The story you tell yourself plays a crucial role in shaping up your life. When what goes on in your head (your story) is centered around a sense of unworthiness and phoniness, you undermine the role of experience and expertise in shaping up your success. Anything good must have been a fluke and anything bad has to do with your own flaws. Positive feedback feels like a mistake and negative feedback, well it only confirms your faults. Others around you seem to be doing well because of their genuine ability, but when you do well they must be overestimating your abilities.

This crippling sense of self-doubt, intellectual inadequacy, and an irrational sense of fear may live in your head, but its consequences aren't limited to your thoughts. They have a very real impact on your life. Not acknowledging your own accomplishments negatively impacts your sense of self-worth. It can make you feel mediocre, unqualified, and incompetent to handle the daily demands and challenges of work life. You may give up on opportunities to avoid the shame and humiliation associated with feelings of failure. Instead of focusing on the good parts of your job, you may fixate on mistakes with the fear that every mistake takes you closer to "being discovered as a fraud."

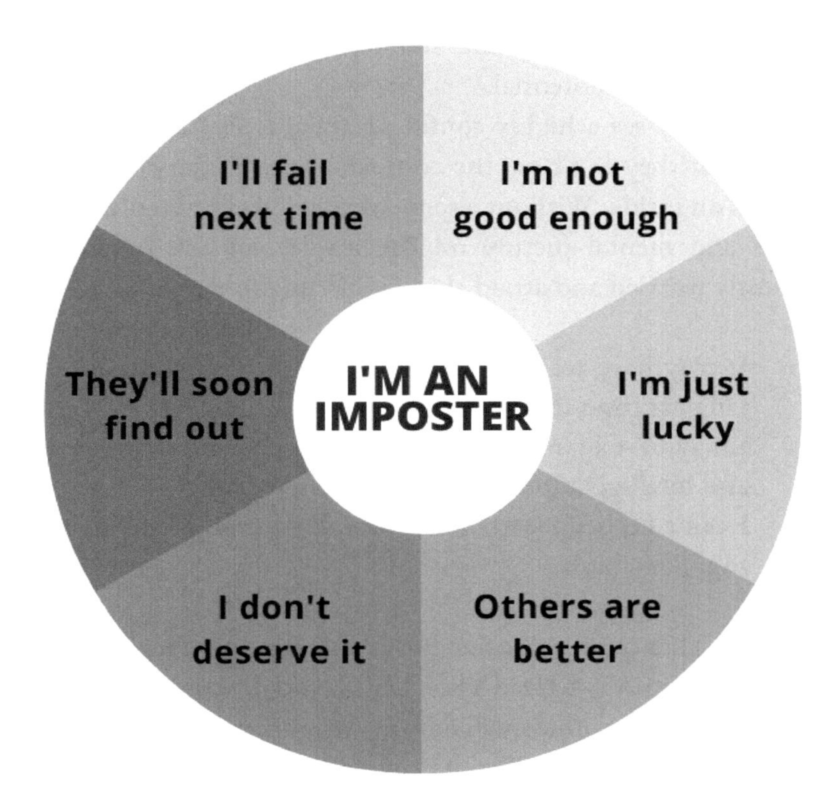

This thing that lives in your head is real and psychologists call it the Imposter Phenomenon or the Imposter Syndrome. First discovered by two psychologists Pauline R. Clance and Suzanne A. Imes in 1978,[1] Imposter Syndrome is the conflict between our sense of who we think we are and who we think we need to be to do well in life and achieve our goals. Denis Waitley, a motivational speaker, and an author puts it best "It's not who you are that holds you back, it's who you think you're not."[2]

Left unhandled, that voice inside your head, your inner critic hijacks your confidence, disqualifies your achievements and instills such a strong sense of failure and rejection that you're willing to sabotage your true potential.

Others may see a highly confident and successful person on the outside, but they can't see the confusion, uncertainty, and conflict that goes on inside. Without a sense of harmony between your image outside and mental picture on the inside, you are bound to be constantly worried and afraid about what might happen...

- It may have worked this time. But they will find out once I fail next time around.
- I may have manipulated them into believing that I am smart and intelligent, but I can't fool them for long.
- I can't keep up with this pretense forever. Someone's going to call my bluff.

Feeling that you are constantly on edge, as though you are winging it is no way to lead a life. Unless you do something about it, your feelings of ineptness will only get magnified. Trying to hide the feelings or push them under the rug will not make them disappear. Being caught up in an imposter cycle will only make things worse.

THE IMPOSTER CYCLE

When self-doubt kicks in from a natural sense of humility about your work, it's healthy. But what if instead of inspiring you to question your choices, it crosses the line and turns into paralyzing fear? When you can't reconcile how you feel about yourself with how the outside world perceives you, it can be incredibly unnerving and throw your balance off a bit. Success makes things even much harder. With every new accomplishment, there's more at stake. Instead of reveling in your success, the realization of the effort you need to put in to keep up with the charade can intensify your fear of discovery.

Amy Cuddy, a social psychologist, and an author writes in her book *Presence*, "Achievements don't stamp out impostor fears. In fact, success can actually make them worse. We can't reconcile a lofty vision of ourselves with our secret knowledge that we don't deserve it. Worldly success introduces us to others who will hold us to a standard we can't possibly meet, thus revealing our true weak, incompetent selves. Achievements present us with new situations and opportunities, which only exacerbate the impostor fears, since every new situation is another proving ground."[3]

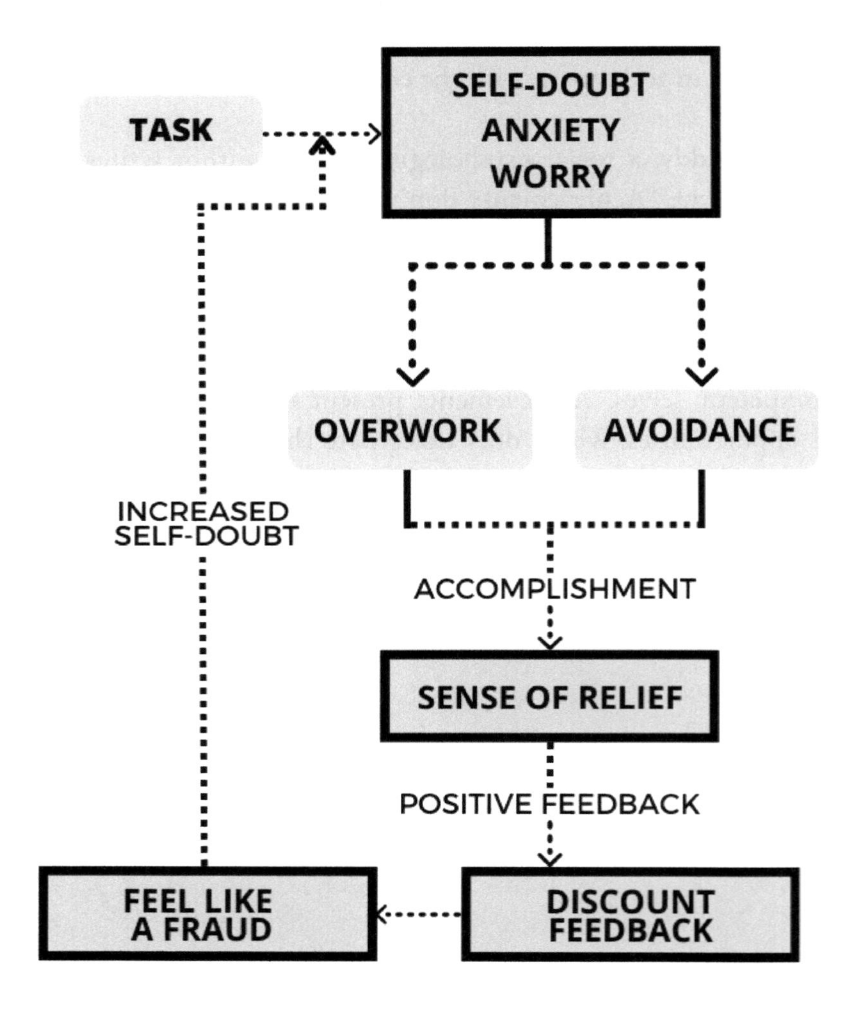

Once self-doubt seeps in, it not only diminishes your accomplishments, it shakes your confidence. Worried about how each mistake reflects on your competence and anxious about not meeting expectations derails you from the goal of "do well and achieve success" to "cover-up and limit exposure."

You either try to make up for your lack of perceived skills by working extra hard or avoid new opportunities by staying under the radar. Overwork and avoidance may be your strategies to get through the day, but take a closer look and you will find that these self-sabotaging behaviors do more damage than good.

Giving up on opportunities that you are well suited to perform limits your potential and working extra hard only leads to exhaustion. And despite your best attempts to avoid exposure, if you do succeed, all the accomplishment only brings a momentary sense of relief. You discount all the positive feedback by attributing it to luck or effort and are back to feeling fraudulent with the belief "I don't deserve this success."

When every project and every assignment seems like a test to be passed, you are never calm or even close to being relaxed. Your imposter cycle starts with self-doubt, but once you are caught inside it, the feeling that your life is on a treadmill just never stops. Irrespective of how many times you push the stop button, the feeling doesn't go away. It's a self-perpetuating cycle that's not only hard to recognize but even harder to break.

This beautiful poem from Katya Ederer captures the feeling well:

Like a boulder chained to your bare ankle
Pulling your fresh thoughts to the dark,
Like a button pushed at a certain angle
She triggers 'rewind' instead of a 'start.'
— Katya Ederer[4]

To bring about any change, a good place to start is to know where you stand right now. What goes on in your head?

Your awareness of how you feel and your willingness to make things better for yourself may be the first step towards creating a better life, but I promise you that the first step is all you need to keep looking forward and never look back.

Unless you make an attempt to learn more about your imposter feelings, you cannot determine the attitudes and behaviors that undermine your confidence and replace them with effective strategies that build it.

Throughout the book, I will give you exercises to help you think deeply about the topic and apply new strategies to put your learning into practice. Remember, to learn and not to do is really not to learn. You can revisit any of these exercises later or repeat them for mastering behaviors that build the confidence to go after the things you desire in your life. All the resources in this book are available online. You can either do these exercises in a notebook or take a printout of the worksheets available online. Download all the resources once and put them to practice as you proceed with the various exercises in this book.

Complete the following exercise to determine what Imposter Syndrome characteristics you demonstrate and identify the thoughts, behaviors, and attitudes that may be pulling you down.

Exercise: What's Your Imposter Score?

Take a moment to read each of the statements below and select the choice that best describes your response using a 5-point scale (1 - Not at all true, 2 - rarely, 3 - sometimes, 4 - often, and 5 - very true). Try to be completely honest. Remember, there are no right or wrong answers. What matters is that you stay true to yourself when you attempt this exercise.

STATEMENT	1	2	3	4	5
Other people think I'm more smart, capable, and confident than I really am.					
Even when others express confidence in my ability, I often worry about not succeeding and doubt that I will do well.					
I tend to magnify mistakes by ignoring the good stuff and dwelling on one negative detail or focusing solely on the part I am unhappy about.					
Whenever I am trusted with a new project, assignment, or responsibility, I'm often afraid and nervous that I may fail even though I have succeeded in the past and generally do well.					
I worry that my peers will find out that I'm not good enough and that I don't deserve to be in this position.					
I have difficulty accepting praise or recognition for my accomplishments.					
I'm afraid that all my success must be some kind of an error and others will discover how much knowledge and ability I really lack.					

I like everything to be 100% perfect otherwise my work won't be good enough.					
I work extremely hard and put in more hours than my peers to avoid being found out that I'm not as capable as they think I am.					
I believe that I received the job or obtained my present position based on qualities such as character or personality and not on experience or skills.					
When people say nice things about me or give me positive feedback, I tend to shrug it aside and discount the importance of everything I have done.					
I see mistakes as a sign of my personal incompetence and try very hard to avoid them or cover them up.					
I sometimes let go of the opportunities to avoid the shame and humiliation associated with failure and the feelings of foolishness.					
I tend to procrastinate by delaying important things or putting them off with the fear that doing a bad job will expose me as a fraud.					
I'm often worried about not performing well and disappointing people who care					

about me by not living up to their expectations of me.					
I avoid being evaluated because I dislike negative feedback and criticism.					
Most of the time, I believe I should have performed better on a project or task than I actually did.					
I often compare my ability to those around me and think they are more competent and intelligent than I am.					
I'm afraid to speak up because I don't want others to realize how little I actually know.					
I believe that I have achieved most of my success not because of my skills and abilities, but due to luck, knowing the right people, or being in the right place at the right time.					

You can download a printable version of "What's Your Imposter Score?" at:
techtello.com/rethink-imposter-syndrome/worksheets/

After marking your response across each statement, sum up your total score across all the responses. Use the table below to identify the intensity of your imposter experience.

Score less than equal to 40	Score between 41 and 60	Score between 61 and 80	Score more than 80
MILD	MODERATE	CONSIDER ABLE	SEVERE

Knowing the intensity of your imposter feelings gives you a peek into your inner experience. Working on the statements and thinking about them helps you realize how those feelings, however real they may seem, are just feelings. You may not have noticed some of the destructive behaviors those feelings tend to evoke earlier, but you can probably see them now.

Mild or severe, your imposter feelings do not make you incompetent. Not feeling capable and confident about yourself just means you're human. Many people struggle with imposter syndrome throughout their life because they refuse to share their vulnerability, but as Brené Brown, a researcher, and an author writes in her book *Daring Greatly* "Vulnerability is not weakness, and the uncertainty, risk, and emotional exposure we face every day are not optional. Our only choice is a question of engagement. Our willingness to own and engage with our vulnerability determines the depth of our courage and the clarity of our purpose; the level to which we protect ourselves from being vulnerable is a measure of our fear and disconnection."[5] Once you own and engage with your imposter feelings in an authentic way, once you stop protecting yourself and practice the courage to be seen, and once you stop being so judgmental about yourself, that's when you'll realize your true worth and experience real transformation from within.

Thinking that everyone else is confident and deserving and you're not is only a delusion. It's easy to make the assumption that others don't engage in fear, insecurity, and self-doubt as you do, but just because you can't see something does not make it true. How you feel is hidden from others just like their feelings are hidden from you. The next chapter will help you see why your imposter feelings are part of a shared experience and not unique. Knowing you aren't alone won't rid you of your imposter feelings, but it sure is comforting to know that others have the same doubts.

Chapter Summary

- Doubting your abilities, attributing your achievements to luck, and thinking that you don't deserve this success diminishes the role of skills and competence in your accomplishments.
- The story you tell yourself plays a crucial role in shaping up your life. When your story is centered around a sense of unworthiness and constant worry that others will find out that you're not good enough, it makes you adopt destructive patterns of behavior to avoid discovery and limit exposure.
- Assuming that everyone around you is more knowledgeable, capable, and competent makes you feel unworthy of your achievements.
- Feeling like an imposter, a sense that you don't belong traps you in a self-perpetuating cycle of self-doubt and self-sabotage behaviors that are hard to recognize and even harder to break.
- Any transformation to overcome these limiting beliefs and

realize your true potential starts with self-awareness. Identify the Imposter Syndrome characteristics you demonstrate and the thoughts, behaviors, and attitudes that may be pulling you down.

- Your imposter feelings do not make you incompetent. It's a sign you're human. Acknowledge and share your vulnerabilities.

CHAPTER 2

Pluralistic Ignorance

IN 2011, DAN ARIELY, Professor of psychology and behavioral economics at Duke University pulled a clever stunt on his undergrads. The students, some of the brightest minds in the country, were there to learn about behavioral economics from the renowned professor.

After asking his students to relax and feel at ease, Ariely started his lecture with a basic question "What is behavioral economics?"[1] And for the next few minutes what he read was a sequence of randomly generated words taken from an engine that's supposed to generate postmodern literature and embedded a few words of his own on capitalism and Adam Smith in it.

Amazed as the packed lecture hall listened attentively and acted normal, he stopped and asked "...and this leads us to the big question. Why has no one asked me what the #$^% am I talking about? Why didn't you stop me when I kept on reading this nonsense for a while? You must have realized that you have no idea what was discussed, but none of you stopped me and the question is why."

Sounds familiar with the meetings and discussions you've been part of?

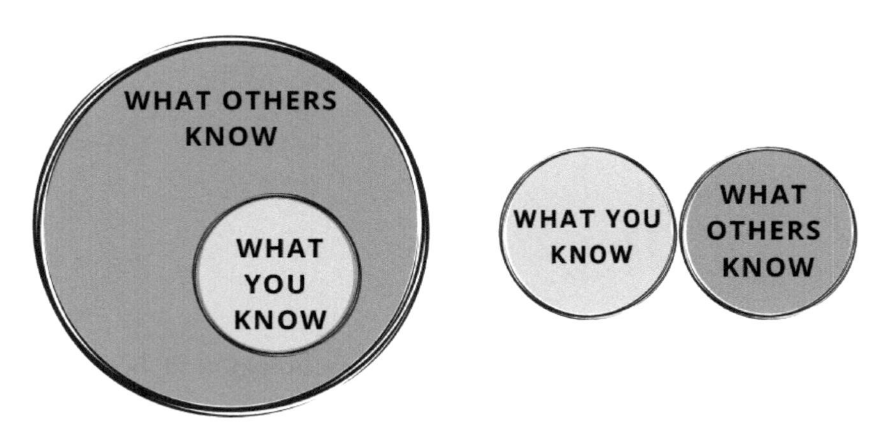

Delusion: Others know 5x more than you

Reality: You know as much as others or more

You've probably experienced this one before:

You're part of a big meeting. An authority figure walks in and delivers a big presentation on the future strategy of your organization. She goes on for a long time explaining the market research, showing fancy graphs, and putting out some big numbers to push her message across. Most of it sounds gibberish to you and doesn't make sense. So you think to yourself "I have no idea what the hell is going on."

Confused and anxious, you look at the people around you. As heads nod in agreement and no one seems to be raising their hands, a feeling of self-doubt kicks in "Am I the only one who doesn't understand this?" Interpreting others' silence as meaning they're on board and feeling you're the only person who has no idea what's going on, you quickly determine that your best option is to keep your mouth shut and not ask any questions. You attempt to hide what you think is your ignorance and incompetence.

YOU THINK YOU ARE ALONE

You're not alone. Everyone else is thinking the same thing. You're simply demonstrating a part of behavior called shared delusion or as psychologists call it pluralistic ignorance. The term was coined by Floyd Henry Allport and his students Daniel Katz and Richard Schanck in the 1930s.[2] Pluralistic ignorance is a psychological state in which you believe that your private thoughts, feelings, beliefs, attitudes, and judgments are different from those of others.

- You doubt yourself, they don't.
- You feel incompetent, they don't.
- You struggle with a project, they don't.

Deluded about other people's real views, you feel compelled to adhere to that delusion. Unable to see what goes on inside other people's heads makes your assumption of what caused your behavior to vary significantly from your interpretation of the same behavior in others.

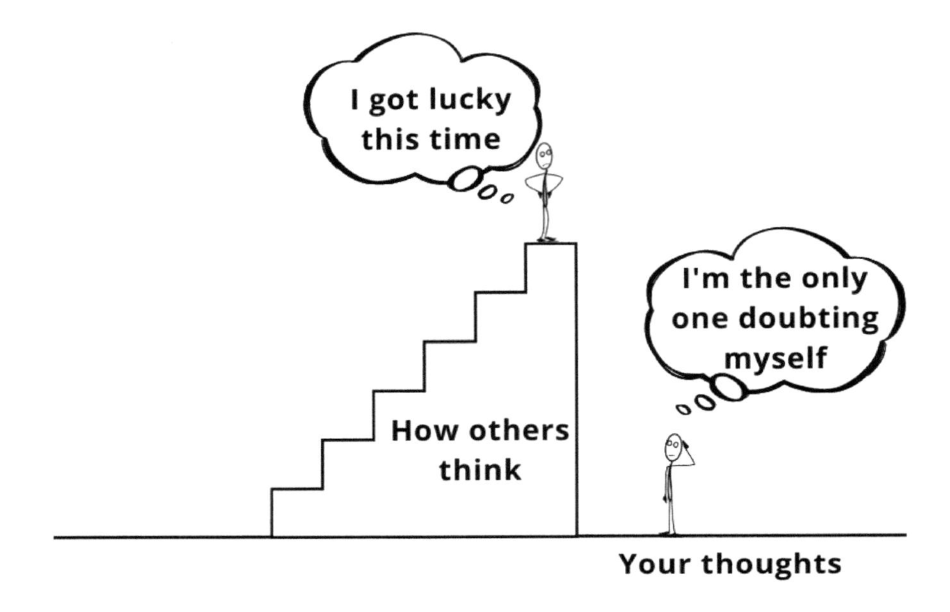

The tape that plays endlessly in your head goes like this:

If *I am the only one with feelings of self-doubt while everyone around me appears confident, then I must be a fraud...I don't belong here...I have fooled them all these years and they all think I'm great but I know better...one of these days they're going to find out.*

It's pluralistic ignorance that magnifies your feelings of being an imposter and makes you think that other people around you are smart and talented and they deserve what they have, but you don't. Thousands of Google searches confirm this: You aren't the only one constantly questioning whether you deserve success or worrying that you're going to be "found out." Research backs it up—70% of individuals experience signs and symptoms of imposter phenomenon at least once in their life.[3]

Millions of people secretly worry they're not as intelligent or as capable as others think they are. Just like you work hard to hide your feelings of being an imposter from others, they do it too.

Highly successful people and those at the top also struggle with feelings of not being good enough. Former Olympic pole vaulter for Australia, Simon Arkell grappled with feeling like an imposter throughout his life.[4] When Simon was going through the ranks as a pole vaulter in Australia, he believed that he was not a talented athlete. He realized as he got better—through just training hard—that if he wanted to succeed, he had to go to the US. He came to the States with a huge chip on his shoulder, no money and he didn't really know anyone. The general opinion where he came from was that there was no way it was ever gonna happen for him. But in 1992 he qualified and made it to the Olympic team, and he was the first Australian to do so in 16 years.

When he got to the Olympics he didn't know many of the Australian athletes and felt like he was in no man's land. Being in the Olympic Village was the hardest and loneliest thing of all. He was competing in the Olympic games but he felt like a total fraud and that he didn't deserve to be there. He said "When I look at people who are really successful, I don't think of them as struggling in any way. I think it looks easy. But for me, everything I've ever done has been the hardest thing I've ever done. Everything has seemed so difficult at the time and as though I've had to try twice as hard as everyone else."

Natalie Portman, the Academy Award-winning actress who attended Harvard from 1999 to 2003 reflected on her experience at the university and her career while speaking at a Harvard event in 2015. She shared how she never felt like she deserved to be at the university during her time and how she still deals with feelings of self-doubt and insecurity "Today I feel much like I did when I came to Harvard Yard as a freshman in 1999...I felt like there had been some mistake, that I wasn't smart enough to be in this company, and that every time I opened my mouth I would have to prove that I wasn't just a dumb actress."[5]

Even the famous Neil Gaiman who has written numerous bestselling novels, comic books, short stories, films, and television screenplays and won major literary awards has publicly discussed his struggles with imposter syndrome. He tells a story from many years ago when he was invited to a gathering of artists and scientists, writers and discoverers of things. He said, "I felt that at any moment they would realise that I didn't qualify to be there, among these people who had really done things."[6]

On his second or third night at the event, Neil Gaiman was standing at the back of the hall and started talking to a very nice, polite, elderly gentleman about several things. That old man pointed to the hall of people, and said "I just look at all these people, and I think, what the heck am I doing here? They've made amazing things. I just went where I was sent." That old man speaking to Neil Gaiman and telling him that "he just went to the moon because he was sent there" was Neil Armstrong. That day Neil Gaiman realized that if Neil Armstrong felt like an imposter, maybe everyone did.

Sheryl Sandberg, Howard Schultz, Tina Fey, David Bowie, Maya Angelou, Tom Hanks, Serena Williams, and numerous other entrepreneurs and celebrities have openly spoken about their experiences with imposter syndrome. Look around and many of your friends, relatives, colleagues, family members, coaches, teachers, and even parents would report feelings of phoniness. This certainly gives credibility to the idea that most of us aren't immune from feeling like a fraudster. You are part of a shared experience and not alone.

So if doubting your skills and abilities is the source of your problem, is building more confidence the answer to dealing with those imposter feelings? As we will see in the next chapter, confidence alone is not sufficient. To do well and achieve success in life, confidence often needs a little dose of another element.

Chapter Summary

- It's true that your thoughts, feelings, and emotions are only visible to you. But it's also true that you make unwarranted conclusions about other people's thoughts in similar situations.
- When being part of a tough project, a challenging discussion, or an important meeting, qualifying others' silence to mean they have understood everything while attributing your own silence to lack of understanding and a desire to fit in makes you fall for shared delusion or as psychologists call it pluralistic ignorance.
- The assumption that others' behavior reflects their genuine skills and abilities while attributing your own behavior to lack of intelligence and competence makes feeling like an imposter a very lonely experience.
- Research on imposter syndrome shows that 70% of people at least once in their life experience such feelings.
- Highly successful people like Sheryl Sandberg, Howard Schultz, Tina Fey, David Bowie, Maya Angelou, Tom Hanks, Serena Williams, Neil Gaiman, Natalie Portman, and numerous others have openly spoken about their experience while living with a sense of ineptness and phoniness.
- Know that whatever you're feeling is part of the shared experience and you're not alone.

CHAPTER 3

Flip Side of Confidence

LACK OF CONFIDENCE or as I call it "The perceived confidence gap" is often attributed to those with imposter syndrome. And while there's some truth to the fact that people with imposter syndrome lack confidence, being fully confident and getting completely rid of self-doubt and insecurity shouldn't be your goal. That's because self-doubt may live on the opposite end of confidence, but being too far on either side can be detrimental to your growth while they are most beneficial when taken in conjunction. Instead of blindly urging for more confidence, what you need is to seek a healthy balance.

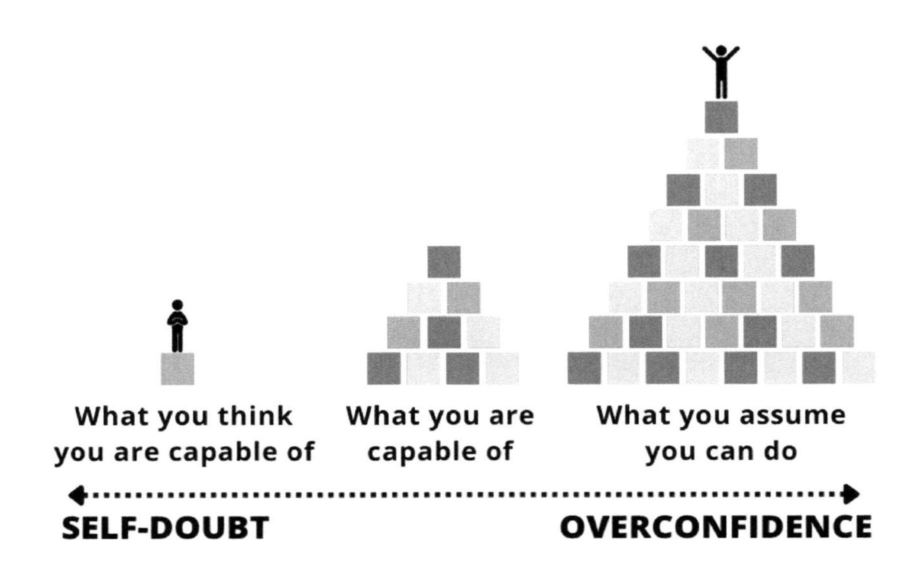

Let's look at the two ends of the confidence spectrum:

1. Self-doubt
2. Overconfidence

Self-doubt

A crippling sense of self-doubt where you constantly wrestle with insecurity and question your abilities or a chronic belief that you're a fraud can confine you inside an invisible box whose edges place a limit on what you can achieve as opposed to your own abilities. The longer you stay inside the box, the more resistant you get to place one foot outside it. The invisible box reinforces your belief that whatever is outside is not meant for you and dissuades you from even reaching for it.

A healthy dose of self-doubt on the other hand can give you the humility to doubt your methods, validate your assumptions, question your knowledge, seek insights from others and work harder on improving your skills. Though some of this doubt can lead to stress and even feelings of fear, it does not make you weak. Instead of crushing your motivation or holding you back, channeling your self-doubt to close your perceived confidence gap can give you just the edge you need to move forward.

Basima Tewfik, assistant professor of Work and Organization Studies at the Massachusetts Institute of Technology who studied the hidden and unexpected upsides of Imposter Syndrome calls it a double-edged sword.[1] She says "Imposter syndrome isn't always good or always bad; it's a much more complex phenomenon than it's been represented to be." She identified that people who lean into feelings of inadequacy and manage them constructively instead of trying to resist or overcome them:

- Are rated more interpersonally effective than their non-imposter peers.
- Are considered to be better collaborators who work well with colleagues.
- Are rated as being more empathetic, and better listeners.
- Are also considered to ask more engaging questions and provide more appealing answers.

Overconfidence

Confidence is absolutely essential to recognize your strengths and get things done. But what happens when you only acknowledge your strengths and refuse to identify your weaknesses or worse you lead with a wrong understanding of your competence often thinking you're more competent than you really are? In other words, you become ignorant of your own ignorance.

A false sense of mastery can promote a strong conviction in your ideas and knowledge. You fail to notice gaps in what you know and refuse to learn what you don't know. You become so eager to speak that you don't stop to observe and listen. You are so blinded by your strengths that you fail to see your weaknesses. You are so consumed in trying to be right that you fail to do the right thing. Driven by the desire to seem more competent, you become blind to your own incompetence—with just enough information, but not enough expertise. Never stopping, never listening, never asking. You leave no space for humility to step in.

Certainty is the biggest monster. Confidence in your knowledge gives you the permission to pass judgment and dismiss information that does not match your beliefs as you feel absolutely certain about your decision. Why would you question your opinion or seek information that contradicts your viewpoint when you are certain of what you know? How can you ever identify the gaps in your knowledge unless you believe it can be flawed?

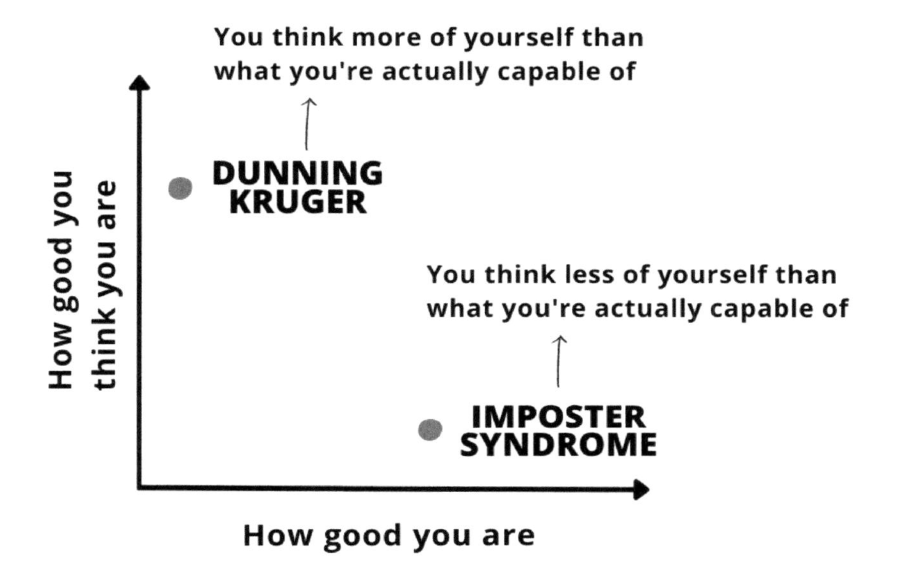

Image adapted from @jessicahagy

Overconfidence creates a sense of superiority and pride in your knowledge that makes you less and less interested in learning and updating your beliefs. Dunning-Kruger effect[2] further clouds your vision of your abilities—the less competent you are, the more you overestimate your abilities. The more you lack competence, the more you are likely to be brimming with overconfidence. Sort of a catch-22. Without the skills to spot your own mistakes, you can't see where you are going wrong and therefore assume you are doing great.

Tim Urban, writer and creator of *Wait But Why* describes arrogance as "ignorance plus conviction." He writes "This is an especially deadly combo because it prevents you from improving. It not only leaves you without real knowledge, it deprives you of the humility needed to gain real knowledge or grow into a better thinker. When you think you are already doing great, you feel like there's no room left for improvement. While humility is a permeable filter that absorbs life experience and converts it into knowledge and wisdom, arrogance is a rubber shield that life experience simply bounces off of."[3]

The right kind of confidence isn't a central point between self-doubt on one end and arrogance on the other. The sweet spot of confidence is tempered with humility.

WHAT YOU NEED IS CONFIDENT HUMILITY

If I ask you to think about confidence, what words come to your mind—power, authority, boldness, worthiness, self-assurance? How about humility—submissive, unassertive, passive, insecure? Many people mistake humility for incompetence or lack of self-confidence. But as C.S. Lewis, one of the intellectual giants of the twentieth century and arguably one of the most influential writers of his day puts it "Humility is not thinking less of yourself, it's thinking of yourself less." It means staying grounded, admitting that you don't know everything, and accepting that you still have a lot to learn.

Confidence, how much you believe in yourself is important. But, humility to know where you fall short and seek help is just as important. What can breed arrogance through unshakeable confidence is avoided by humility.

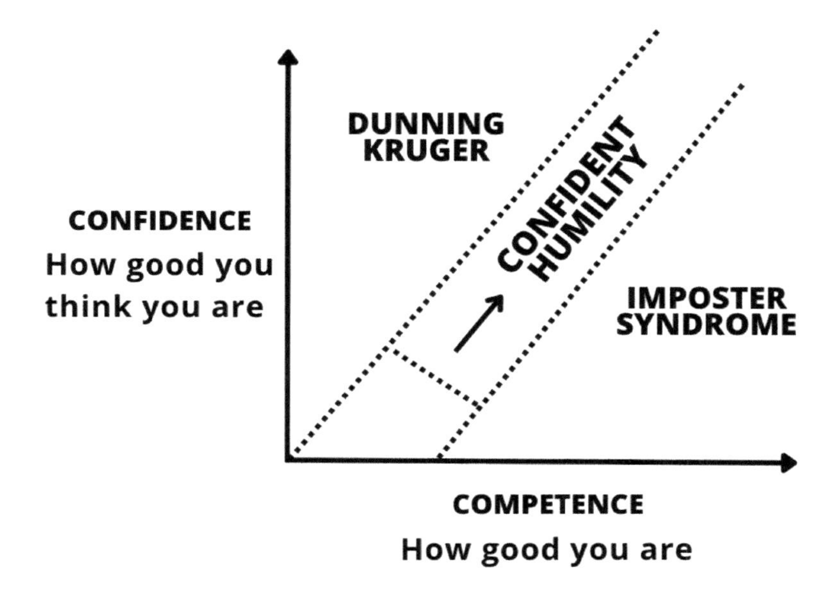

Confident humility is:

- Confidence in your ability to make the right decision while acknowledging that you need others to do it right.
- Knowing what you don't know and having trust in what you do.
- Having faith in your strengths, while also being aware of your weaknesses.
- Accepting that you don't have the required knowledge, but enough confidence in your ability to acquire that knowledge.

Adam Grant, an organizational psychologist, and professor at the Wharton School of Business at the University of Pennsylvania describes it in his book *Think Again* as "having faith in our capability while appreciating that we may not have the right solution or even be addressing the right problem. That gives us enough doubt to reexamine our old knowledge and enough confidence to pursue new insights."[4]

Whitney Wolfe Herd is the world's youngest self-made female billionaire and the perfect exemplar of confident humility. As co-founder and vice president of marketing at Tinder, she was already part of a great business success story. But that didn't end quite so well for her. After resigning from Tinder in 2014, she founded Bumble, a dating app. It was her confidence that guided her to compete against Tinder and her humility that allowed her to question the needs of the dating space. Her experience from Tinder was useful. But, what really played out in her success story was her ability to question that knowledge. She defied previous dating norms and decided to let women make the first move in the app. Even though 90% of dating startups fail, she carved out a lucrative space by focusing on the needs of one segment: women. "Let's change thousands of years of behavior. Globally," she said.[5]

Robert Iger, former CEO of Disney is another ideal example of confident humility. In his book *The Ride of a Lifetime*, he writes about how he felt when he first accepted the role to be the president of ABC entertainment. It was the first time in the history of the company that the person running ABC Entertainment wasn't from the entertainment world "It wasn't quite leaping without a parachute, but it felt a lot like free fall at first. I told myself: You have a job. They're expecting you to turn this business around. Your inexperience can't be an excuse for failure."[6]

He describes how confident humility looked like for someone like him who didn't know much about the business at the time "So what do you do in a situation like that? The first rule is not to fake anything. You have to be humble, and you can't pretend to be someone you're not or to know something you don't. You're also in a position of leadership, though, so you can't let humility prevent you from leading...It's a fine line, and something I preach today. You have to ask the questions you need to ask, admit without apology what you don't understand, and do the work to learn what you need to learn as quickly as you can. There's nothing less confidence-inspiring than a person faking knowledge they don't possess. True authority and true leadership come from knowing who you are and not pretending to be anything else."

Building confidence isn't about faking competence or pretending to know something you don't. It's about recognizing that you are indeed capable, believing in the abilities you truly have, and not being afraid to utilize those talents.

Complete the following exercise to apply confident humility to your past experiences where you struggled with self-doubt or lead with overconfidence.

Exercise: Apply Confident Humility

Think about the two different scenarios described below and try to remember an instance where your behavior matched these scenarios. It could be at your work or in your role as a parent, spouse, community helper, friend, teacher, coach...just about anybody.

Scenario 1: A crippling sense of self-doubt which created a fear of failure so deep that it prevented you from taking up the right opportunities or pursuing your goals.

Scenario 2: Overconfidence which prevented you from seeing the gaps in your own knowledge, made you too self-assured to question your assumptions or ask questions and made you ignore other people's opinions.

Examples of some situations:

- An opportunity to lead a big project
- Presenting your work in front of a large group
- Making a decision to invest in a new idea
- Giving an interview

Picture these instances as vividly in your mind as you can. Try to remember what happened when you behaved this way. How did you feel? What did you do afterward? What impact did it have on your life? Given an opportunity to do it again, how can you apply confident humility next time? Now, write them down. Do this for each scenario.

1. Describe the instance in detail. What happened?

____

____

2. How did you feel?

____

____

3. What did you do afterward?

____

____

4. What impact did it have on your life?

____

____

5. Given an opportunity to do it again, how can you apply confident humility next time?

____

____

You can download a printable version of "Apply Confident Humility" at:
techtello.com/rethink-imposter-syndrome/worksheets/

If you are wondering about how to apply confident humility without any strategies on actually building your confidence, don't worry for now. We will explore strategies to build confidence in later chapters. For now know that the purpose of this exercise wasn't to build your confidence, but to help you visualize the benefits of applying confident humility in day-to-day problems.

Knowing that your imposter thoughts aren't necessarily a bad thing and a little bit of self-doubt shields your confidence from turning into arrogance, you can use them as fuel to fill gaps in your knowledge and consider them as an opportunity to acknowledge your strengths while practicing humility to recognize your limits too.

Imposter syndrome only shows up in certain situations and isn't part of your thoughts and feelings all the time. Whenever doing something difficult—a step up from the current role, signing up for a complex task or a project, shifting between jobs, presenting your ideas in front of a large group—you need to take a step outside your comfort zone. The fear of not knowing how to do something and the uncertainty of the outcome makes you doubt your abilities and question whether you're right in taking up this challenge. But, as we will learn in the next chapter, embracing this discomfort and leaving your zone of comfort is essential to do anything significant. The objective of your expanded comfort zone is to reach an optimal level where your skills increase and you become comfortable with a new level of challenge without crossing the boundaries in an unproductive manner which leads to intense anxiety and makes you scared to try new things in the future.

Chapter Summary

- Many people either err on the side of confidence without competence (overconfidence leading to arrogance) or competence without the confidence to put their ideas into action (excessive self-doubt leading to imposter thoughts).
- Instead of trying to rid yourself of self-doubt, think of self-doubt as a necessary component to build and practice the right kind of confidence.
- While a crippling sense of self-doubt can prevent you from taking action, a healthy dose of self-doubt motivates you to learn, ask better questions, and challenge your assumptions. When channeled right, this self-doubt does not pull you back. Rather, it serves as fuel to propel you into positive action.
- Having excessive confidence in your skills and abilities without the humility to doubt your methods can turn your

ignorance into arrogance. Confidence, how much you believe in yourself is important. But, humility to know where you fall short and seek help is just as important.

- The right kind of confidence isn't a central point with self-doubt on one end and overconfidence on the other. The sweet spot of confidence is tempered with humility.
- You don't need confidence. What you need is confident humility—having confidence in your knowledge and skills while knowing that it isn't sufficient to get everything right; acknowledging your strengths while recognizing your limits too.

CHAPTER 4

A Step Outside Your Comfort Zone

IMAGINE YOU never have to step outside your comfort zone and all the responsibilities you need to fulfill align perfectly with your skills and abilities—you have the confidence to present your ideas, the courage to confront difficult situations at work, competence to tackle big projects, skills to get past every major obstacle and turn every opportunity into triumph; no place for self-doubt to kick in and no imposter thoughts to live with.

Pretty great, right?

Without the difficulty that comes with not knowing how to do something or the challenge to stretch your skills and test your abilities, would you really learn and grow? Will your work be meaningful and keep you motivated if everything came easy to you?

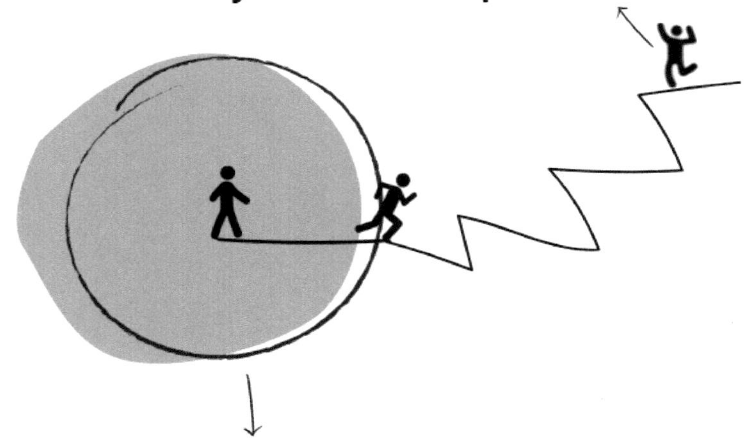

You can't sit inside your comfort zone and expect great things to happen. Your comfort zone may be the place where you feel capable and at ease, but stretching outside your comfort zone in most cases is the only way to achieve your goals. Yes, it's terrifying. Yes, it will be uncomfortable. But, you have to be comfortable being uncomfortable. Taking risks, facing your fears, embracing challenges, and sticking with difficult tasks may cause some discomfort in the moment, but it is what leads to growth in the long run.

The cost of our ever-shrinking comfort zone, social science writer John W. Gardner argues, is tremendous. In his book *Self-Renewal*, he writes about the role of failure in learning and growth "We pay a heavy price for our fear of failure. It is a powerful obstacle to growth. It assures the progressive narrowing of the personality and prevents exploration and experimentation. There is no learning without some difficulty and fumbling. If you want to keep on learning, you must keep on risking failure — all your life. It's as simple as that."[1]

Your imposter thoughts do not strike within the confines and constraints of your "perceived competence." When you refuse every opportunity to explore your potential and put a limit on possible options, your risk of being exposed may go significantly down but your behavior also gives you the permission to disqualify everything you have achieved so far and diminish all your own accomplishments.

What's there to feel like a fraud if you:

- Never got a promotion
- Never had to confront difficult situations
- Never made a job switch
- Never asked to lead a team
- Never needed to network
- Never signed up for a complex task
- Never expected to present your ideas to a large group
- Never given an opportunity to handle a big responsibility
- Never had to pitch an important project to a client
- Never expected to perform a task that's a step-up from the current role

It's the thought of leaving the comfort zone that makes you nervous and challenges you to question your capability and competence. It's the unfamiliar that's scary which makes you doubt your abilities. It's the risk that comes with stepping into the unknown that makes you worry about not meeting others' expectations.

When expected to perform in a situation that's a bit outside your comfort zone, it's hard not to focus on the potential impact of failure. Confronting your imposter feelings can be debilitating and the risk of falling short and being declared inadequate can be quite unnerving and unsettling.

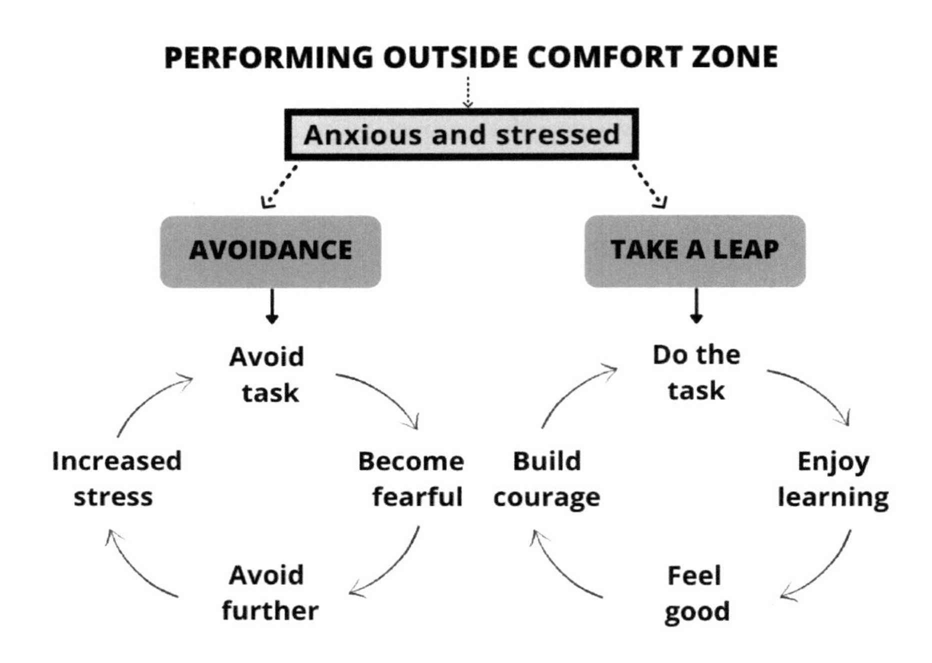

It's in these moments that you need to make a decision:

Option 1: Avoidance - Reject opportunities that require you to stretch, and save yourself from any potential failure and harm. Thinking that you don't have what it takes creates a negative cycle of fear and avoidance—you feel anxious and stressed about performing outside your comfort zone, actively avoid it, become more and more fearful about taking the leap, and continue to avoid it further leading to more anxiety and stress. **Consequence:** Less learning and growth; short-term relief; long-term leads to more anxiety and stress.

Option 2: Take a leap - Embrace the opportunities that may seem uncomfortable at first, and turn them into learning and development goals. Not letting your anxiety get in the way creates a positive cycle of useful action—you may start off feeling anxious and stressed about performing outside your comfort zone, decide to take the leap, enjoy learning, growth, and experimentation along the way, feel good about taking this chance, and build the courage to do it again next time around. **Consequence**: More learning and growth; reduced anxiety with the benefit of acquiring courage and conviction to make things happen.

You can either maintain flawed beliefs about yourself and hold onto your self-doubt or you can do the thing that scares you only to discover the joy and reward that comes from going after the things you dreaded for so long. When struggling to make this decision for yourself, remember this from Eleanor Roosevelt, the first lady of the United States from 1933 to 1945 "You gain strength, courage, and confidence by every experience in which you really stop to look fear in the face. You are able to say to yourself, 'I lived through this horror. I can take the next thing that comes along.' You must do the thing you think you cannot do."[2]

However, be cautious. The best way to make progress isn't to push yourself as hard as possible and way beyond the bounds of your comfort. That will only leave you defeated and exhausted.

STRETCHING YOURSELF WITHOUT GOING TOO FAR

Melody Wilding, an author and a coach tells a story of how relentlessly pushing her comfort zone led her straight to burnout.[3] Most mornings, as she crammed on a bus heading out of New York City, with a two-hour commute ahead of her, stress-induced cortisol was the only thing keeping her from collapsing in exhaustion. She writes "Up to this point in my life, I had been driven by a mentality of pushing harder: straight As in school, top of my class in college, and now a demanding job in Manhattan. On the outside, everything looked peachy—as if I were a picture of success. On the inside, I was feeling defeated and helpless. In accordance with the self-improvement mindset, I rationalized these feelings as stemming from my own inadequacy. If I felt I was juggling more than I possibly could, I clearly had to hustle more. I just need to work harder, I told myself. I'm out of my comfort zone. It'll get better. I'll adjust."

Did she? No.

Instead of improving, as the months went on, her sense of dread grew "Every day was a cocktail of fear. What crisis would crop up? What new project would be dropped into my lap this morning? My health was crumbling. Facing my fear should have allowed me to grow, as I understood the motivational slogans. Instead, in my mid-twenties, I found myself laid up in bed, so tired I could barely move, and suffering from heart palpitations and nightmares. By pushing myself in the name of getting uncomfortable, I had self-sacrificed to the point of exhaustion."

Contrast this with the story of Adam Grant, an organizational psychologist and professor at the Wharton School of Business at the University of Pennsylvania who overcame his fear of public speaking by stepping outside his comfort zone. Years ago he was invited to give his first public speech as a student. It was a terrifying experience "For weeks beforehand, I had nightmares about forgetting my lines, waking up in a cold sweat. No matter how much I practiced, for the three days leading up to the speech, I could hardly breathe."[4]

However, he decided to step outside his comfort zone—he gave the speech and nothing went terribly wrong. Since then he has given hundreds of public speeches and presentations. He still gets nervous occasionally, but public speaking is now one of his favorite activities.

Why did Melody Wilding fail while Adam Grant succeeded in pushing outside his comfort zone?

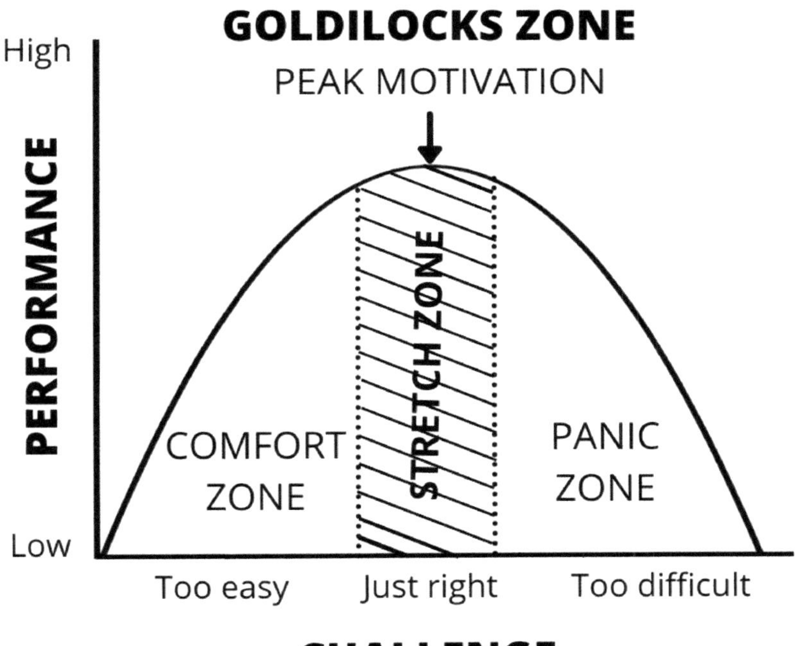

To understand this, let's go to Andy Molinsky, a professor of organizational behavior at Brandeis University's International Business school who describes three zones when it comes to comfort:[5]

Comfort zone: Comfort zone is when you're in a familiar situation and are experiencing very little anxiety.

Stretch zone: A stretch zone is when you're experiencing some level of anxiety, but at a point where you can turn it into motivation and productivity fuel.

Panic zone: You enter a panic zone when the threshold overtakes your capacity to handle it.

Melody was operating in her panic zone which made her crumble under the pressure and demands of her job while Adam Grant was working in his stretch zone which enabled him to learn, push ahead and get better.

The Stretch Zone is your zone of optimal development when working on tasks that are of manageable difficulty. Manageable difficulty rids you of feeling bored with tasks that are easy for you while not getting frustrated when it far exceeds your current abilities. Mihaly Csikszentmihalyi, a psychologist noted for his work in the study of happiness and creativity found that "Enjoyment appears at the boundary between boredom and anxiety, when the challenges are just balanced with the person's capacity to act."[6] Also called Goldilocks Rule, named after the fairy tale Goldilocks and the three bears, the rule states that human beings experience peak motivation when working on tasks that are right on the edge of their current abilities. Neither too easy nor too difficult. Just right.[7] In other words, when taking a step outside your comfort zone, it's important to seek just the right level of difficulty.

Let's say you have to present your ideas in front of senior leaders in the organization. You will obviously be stressed about doing it right. To work within your stretch zone without entering your panic zone, this is what you need to do: use your knowledge and skills to prepare the material, practice speaking up multiple times, take help from colleagues, and try to anticipate their questions ahead of time. By doing a lot of work upfront, you will perform well by staying within your stretch zone while avoiding your panic zone which will make you quit.

A key thing to remember when stepping out of your comfort zone is this: everyone's reaction to stress is different. My stretch zone could well be your panic zone. When entering this area of productive discomfort, be willing to experiment, evaluate and readjust your position. Openness, flexibility, and curiosity are as important as effort, strategy, persistence, and willingness to take risks. Knowing yourself better by discovering the sweet spot of your stretch zone is the only way to make progress and set yourself up for success without going crazy in the process.

Let's do this exercise to learn more about your strategies to avoid stepping outside your comfort zone. Knowing how you behave when confronted with difficult situations will help you master the new behaviors we will learn later to get over your self-limiting beliefs and build the courage to take action.

Exercise: Identify Your Avoidance Strategies

Acting outside your comfort zone isn't easy and your imposter feelings make it all the more difficult for you to recognize destructive patterns of behavior which limit your learning and growth as you avoid acting outside it.

Read the questions below and write down your responses to identify the specific ways in which you might be limiting yourself.

1. Think about a situation or a task that's critical for your job or career that you have been avoiding? Describe it.

 ____

 ____

2. What thoughts and feelings made you avoid the task?

 ____

 ____

3. What was your avoidance strategy—denying the opportunity altogether, doing only a part of the job that was easy and leaving the uncomfortable parts, procrastinating by putting it off for so long that it negatively affected the outcomes you achieved or delegating it even though it was something you should have done on your own? If you applied any other strategy, write that down.

 ____

 ____

4. What impact did it have on your growth?

____

____

5. How frequently do you tend to avoid stepping outside your comfort zone—not at all, rarely, sometimes, often?

____

____

You can download a printable version of "Identify Your Avoidance Strategies" at:
techtello.com/rethink-imposter-syndrome/worksheets/

Knowing what you now know, can you clearly see that staying inside your comfort zone does not protect you? Being trapped within your comfort zone magnifies your imposter feelings as it takes away your ability to do anything that will make you question those limiting beliefs or explore alternative views. A step outside your comfort zone is all you need to see for yourself that your imposter feelings are just a creation of your mind and not something real.

Do you wonder though why you feel this way? Your imposter feelings may live inside your head, but they didn't originate there. In the next chapter, we will trace back the source of your imposter feelings to your own personal history. Messages about success, failure, and mistakes given to you as a child, the culture of your organization, and certain stereotypes can plant the seeds of self-doubt which can later manifest into feelings of ineptness and unworthiness.

Chapter Summary

- Your comfort zone is the place where you feel at ease. Doing things you have always done is less scary, but limiting your options and staying within the zone leaves less opportunities for learning and hardly any room for growth.
- Your growth is one step outside your comfort zone. Embracing the discomfort and facing your fears is the only way to utilize your knowledge, gain new skills and build the courage to look beyond your self-perceived limitations to identifying and acknowledging your unique talents.
- Given an opportunity to do something new, you can either give in to your fears and try to avoid it thereby increasing anxiety when presented with further opportunities or you can take the leap and do the thing thereby building the courage and conviction to make things happen.
- When leaving your comfort zone, aim to enter a *stretch zone* by working on tasks that are right on the edge of your current abilities. Neither too easy nor too difficult. Just right. A little bit of anxiety in the stretch zone is exactly what you need to stay productive and feel motivated to take action.
- You enter a panic zone when the challenge of doing something crosses the boundary of productive discomfort and far exceeds your capability to handle it. Avoid it at all costs.
- Identify the sweet spot of your stretch zone through experimentation, evaluation, and adjustment. Expanding

your comfort zone by working within your stretch zone will give you the confidence to take on new challenges without letting your self-doubt get in the way of achieving success at work and in life.

CHAPTER 5

Imposter Origin Story

WHAT MAKES you doubt yourself? When did these feelings of unworthiness, undeserving and not being good enough started? Was there a specific event in your life that triggered them or were the seeds of self-doubt planted slowly in your mind? I have asked myself these questions many times. Looking back at my personal history led me to a path where I was able to understand myself better and channel this newfound information to confront my feelings of being inadequate and identify ways to move forward without letting those feelings pull me down.

Your personal history is not the same as mine. Your personality, where you grew up, how you were raised, your experiences, your workplace, and even your gender, ethnicity, and race plays a critical role in shaping up your beliefs. You need to look back at your history to determine when did the feeling of not being good enough begin and where your beliefs that you're less capable and worthy came from? Knowing how your imposter thoughts came into being is a useful source to pause, step aside from assuming you're right in feeling this way to challenging those thoughts.

Your beliefs are not entirely a result of your personality

Many factors play a role in shaping up those beliefs

As much as you like to believe that your imposter feelings are solely a result of your disposition and personality, many factors outside of you play a major role in spurring up those negative feelings. In order to gain a complete understanding of your imposter feelings, you need to take into account environmental, social, cultural, and other contextual factors that made you internalize negative perceptions of yourself and question your abilities.[1]

Dr. Carolyn Teschke, molecular and cell biology professor and Associate Department Head of Undergraduate Research and Education at the University of Connecticut, principal investigator of a National Institutes of Health (NIH)-funded viral assembly research program and author of more than 50 peer-reviewed articles shared her first encounter with Imposter Syndrome.

Teschke traced back her feelings of inadequacy to her undergraduate years. A few unpleasant experiences like being yelled at by a laboratory course instructor and being humiliated by a seminar speaker, in both cases for simply asking a question left her feeling mortified. She carried those experiences with her through her graduate and postdoctoral training "I never asked a question in a seminar my entire time in grad school and rarely asked a question in classes. I was afraid I would ask something stupid and that would negatively impact me with my first advisor."[2] The feelings hit her professional life once she became a professor as she constantly worried about whether she is qualified enough to know the answer to her students' questions. It wasn't Teschke's personality that made her doubt herself, but a few bad social encounters that impacted a big part of her life.

Rana el Kaliouby grew up in a traditional Egyptian family. She left Egypt and came to the UK for her PhD at the University of Cambridge. After Cambridge, she worked at MIT as a research scientist where she spearheaded applications in emotion recognition technology, specializing in mental health and Autism. It was here that el Kaliouby first had the idea of using artificial intelligence to analyze and understand human emotions. With a plan to develop technology that understands humans, the way that we understand each other, she went on to co-found Affectiva in 2009 with fellow MIT scholar Professor Rosalind Picard.[3]

Despite all her accomplishments, el Kaliouby had no faith in her ability to lead. "I was a woman in a foreign country with no business experience, working in a field that is to this day overwhelmingly white and male. How could I be an executive? I told myself I couldn't, and we opted to hire a seasoned business executive to serve as CEO."[4]

A few years later when the CEO left, board members recommended Kaliouby to step into the role, but she had a lot of doubts "I'd never been a CEO before, so how could I take this on? The voice in my head told me I can't, I shouldn't and that I'd fail."

She was surprised to see Affectiva's head of sales raise his hand to take the job, despite never having been a CEO either. It was at that moment that el Kaliouby realized that women often don't raise their hand unless they check all of the boxes "I sat down and thought about what a CEO does—and what I was doing—I realised I was not only ready for the job, but I was already doing it. I summoned my courage, approached the executive team and the board, and ultimately stepped into the role."

Years later, el Kaliouby does not consider herself free of self-doubt "Sometimes I still hear the 'Debbie Downer' voice in my head. But I have learned to reframe the message. It is now my advocate, not my adversary, challenging me to move forward out of my comfort zone."

It wasn't el Kaliouby's personality but her upbringing as a 'nice Egyptian girl' combined with stereotyping and lack of representation of female leaders at the top that filled her head with self-doubt.

WHY DO YOU FEEL LIKE AN IMPOSTER?

Your beliefs not only determine how you navigate the world and the things in it, they also feed into everything you do. They are central to shaping up your experiences and determining how you operate in your life. The more you latch onto these beliefs, the more they control you.

For example:

- Your belief that you aren't good enough can cause you to give up on anything that's even a little outside your comfort zone.

- Your belief that others have made a mistake in considering you for this title or position can make you downplay your achievements.
- Your belief that others are more capable and intelligent than you can lead to feelings of low self-esteem.

You may already have a good idea of the beliefs you hold about yourself, but do you know where they came from? Let's look into 3 primary causes of your imposter feelings:

1. Shaped by nature and nurture
2. Influenced by organization culture
3. Pigeonholed by stereotypes

Shaped by nature and nurture

Your experiences as a child have a profound impact on how you view yourself and others. Your parents and other adults close to you like your teachers, coaches, grandparents, aunts, and uncles significantly influenced your belief system and it's these early experiences that determine how you experience various things and how capable and competent you feel now. Small seeds of self-doubt planted into your childhood may grow inside you and continue with you to college, graduate school, and then your work.

Your individual personality traits can definitely make you more prone to stress and anxiety, or you may have a family history with anxiety and depression leading to negative thought patterns and self-doubt,[5] but equally important are the messages you received as a child. Your everyday interactions, beliefs, ideas, and opinions from those close to you laid the foundation for your personal belief system—the things they said to you, the views they shared, their expectations of you, and how they viewed achievement and accomplishment. Much like everything else you learned as a child, if you internalized these messages without questioning them, they become a part of your self. You come to rely on them, letting them control the way you think and also how you act.

Think about these different kinds of messages that may have been passed to you as a child:

Negative and discouraging: Negative messaging from parents can crush confidence early in life and haunt you throughout your personal and professional life. Being compared to your friends and siblings and told that "you're not good enough" or that "you will never be as good as them" sticks with you. Taking your parents' view of yourself as a source of truth discourages you from feeling good about yourself and makes you dismiss your accomplishments.

Conditional on performance: As a child, you were wired to seek approval from your parents. What if your parents' approval was conditional on your performance—showering you with love and showing interest in you when you performed well while being angry and uninterested when you did not do so well? With good grades and high academic achievements[6] being the primary focus, you learn to rely only on exceptional performance as the true measure of your worth.

Undeserved praise or no praise at all: Being raised in a family where it wasn't considered appropriate to talk about achievements or having parents who never praised you irrespective of how well you performed can impact your self-esteem, and breed deep insecurity making it much harder for you to internalize your accomplishments. Lack of praise certainly hits you hard as a child, but equally negative is the undeserving praise. When you're applauded for skills you don't possess or deemed remarkable for things you aren't good at, it instills a sense of phoniness that stays with you throughout life.

Conflicted about achievement: When how your parents viewed achievement varied significantly from how other important people in your life (teacher, coach) defined it, it's difficult to rationalize how you were doing. For example, your parents might have viewed being top of the class as the only measure of being smart while your teacher thought you were brilliant even when you didn't score the highest in each subject. Inconsistent messages like these can create a conflict between feeling good about yourself for doing well to feeling not so great assuming you are only doing a mediocre job.

Focus on innate talent: If you grew up in a household where innate intellectual ability mattered more, you learn to rely on natural talent as a measure of success as opposed to the role of hard work, effort, and perseverance in shaping up your life. This distorted view about talent and ability made you assume that everything should come easy to you if you're talented. You conclude: If you need to put in the effort or need to work hard at something, you must not be talented. This view about yourself leads to imposter feelings the moment you find something difficult to do, or face a challenge.

Labels given to you by others: As a child, you might have been assigned labels based on certain traits—smart, talented, clever, bright, sensitive, hardworking, athletic, not creative. Internalizing these labels and using them as a measure of your worth often leads to imposter feelings later. If your sibling was labeled smart while you were labeled hardworking, you may come to think less of yourself and use hard work as your strategy to make up for your perceived lack of talent. On the other hand, if you were labeled smart, you may find it hard to keep up with the expectations and any sign of failure or mistakes can make you doubt your abilities or consider yourself incompetent.

Thinking about the messages you received as a child and knowing the crucial role they play in shaping up your beliefs gives you the opportunity to question them instead of treating them as your source of truth. Even a small step towards identifying the beliefs that may not be right for you opens a new world of possibilities that seemed impossible earlier, but now appear perfectly within your reach.

Influenced by organization culture

Work is where you spend most of your waking hours as an adult. It's possible that you may bring your own sense of inadequacy to the workplace. But it's also quite possible that the leaders and the culture of your organization contribute to your feelings of imposter syndrome. You may enter the workplace feeling confident and competent, but the specific dynamics of your work environment can plant the seeds for imposter syndrome to flourish.

No doubt you want to work in an environment that values and recognizes your contributions. But what if instead of fostering confidence, the workplace culture makes you feel invalidated, unappreciated and reinforces your insecurities by making you feel that you don't belong?

Here are some signs of a toxic work culture that may cultivate and sustain a sense of phoniness:

- Made to feel stupid or inept for asking questions.
- Saying "I don't know" or admitting a gap in knowledge is looked down upon as a sign of incompetence.
- Asking for help signals that you're unqualified and unfit for the job.
- Mistakes are punished, making you work hard towards a flawless execution to prove to others that you belong.
- Unrealistic goals and expectations make you feel inadequate for not doing a good job.
- Expected to prove yourself over and over again creating a belief that you're only as good as your last project.
- An insecure boss who micromanages and nitpicks your work making you feel inadequate at all times.
- A highly competitive environment that encourages practices to outshine others and keeps you on your toes making you feel that you're never good enough.
- 24/7 connected culture where you are expected to work late, always be on and available at all times creating the need to work harder than others to prove your worth.
- Uncertainty about the work performance due to lack of feedback on how you're doing causes you to doubt yourself and feel insecure about the job.
- Constantly shifting performance objectives and goals make it difficult for you to know if you are meeting expectations causing you to be concerned about being exposed as a fraud and feeling incompetent.

When you work in an environment where you're rarely acknowledged for your contributions, where you're constantly reminded of things you aren't good at as opposed to shining a light on your strengths, where you find it hard to keep up with the pace of unrealistic expectations, where you're expected to obsess about your mistakes as opposed to celebrating your accomplishments, where at the end of each day instead of feeling happy about adding value you feel relieved that you weren't exposed and no one discovered you're incompetent, that workplace feeds your insecurities, destroys your self-confidence and makes it harder for you to realize that it's your imposter feelings that are fake and it's not you.

Pigeonholed by stereotypes

Christy Pichichero, an author and professor of history at George Mason University shared her first experience with imposter syndrome when she was accepted into Princeton. When a classmate angrily accused her of getting in only because she was Black, she believed it "I sort of internalized this assumption that came from other people that no level of accomplishment by a Black girl could open the doors of the aptly named Ivory Tower, that only affirmative action could do that. And so, from that point on, I really did start to doubt myself. Could Princeton have made a mistake? Perhaps I was a fraud. And these thoughts really plagued me throughout college and into my years as a professor."[7] Christy calls it discriminatory gaslighting which happens when dominant social groups use psychological tricks to maintain their power and privilege by sowing self-doubt and dependence in minoritized groups.

Maureen Zappala, a former propulsion engineer who worked at NASA for 13 years shared her own struggles with self-doubt "I thought they only hired me because they need more women. I wasn't a straight-A student, so I didn't think it was my transcript that opened the door. Terrified of failing, I worked harder than I thought possible. I believed if people saw my hard work, they wouldn't notice I didn't belong."[8]

Christy Pichichero and Maureen Zappala aren't exceptions. Research shows that women and people from ethnic minorities are subject to persistent negative stereotyping[9] causing them to doubt their abilities and feel out of place. Dan Ariely, author of *Predictably Irrational* explains how stereotyping influences our behavior "Expectations also shape stereotypes. A stereotype, after all, is a way of categorizing information, in the hope of predicting experiences. The brain cannot start from scratch at every new situation. It must build on what it has seen before. For that reason, stereotypes are not intrinsically malevolent. They provide shortcuts in our never-ending attempt to make sense of complicated surroundings. This is why we have the expectation that an elderly person will need help using a computer or that a student at Harvard will be intelligent. But because a stereotype provides us with specific expectations about members of a group, it can also unfavorably influence both our perceptions and our behavior."[10]

He adds "Research on stereotypes shows not only that we react differently when we have a stereotype of a certain group of people, but also that stereotyped people themselves react differently when they are aware of the label that they are forced to wear (in psychological parlance, they are "primed" with this label). One stereotype of Asian-Americans, for instance, is that they are especially gifted in mathematics and science. A common stereotype of females is that they are weak in mathematics. This means that Asian-American women could be influenced by both notions."

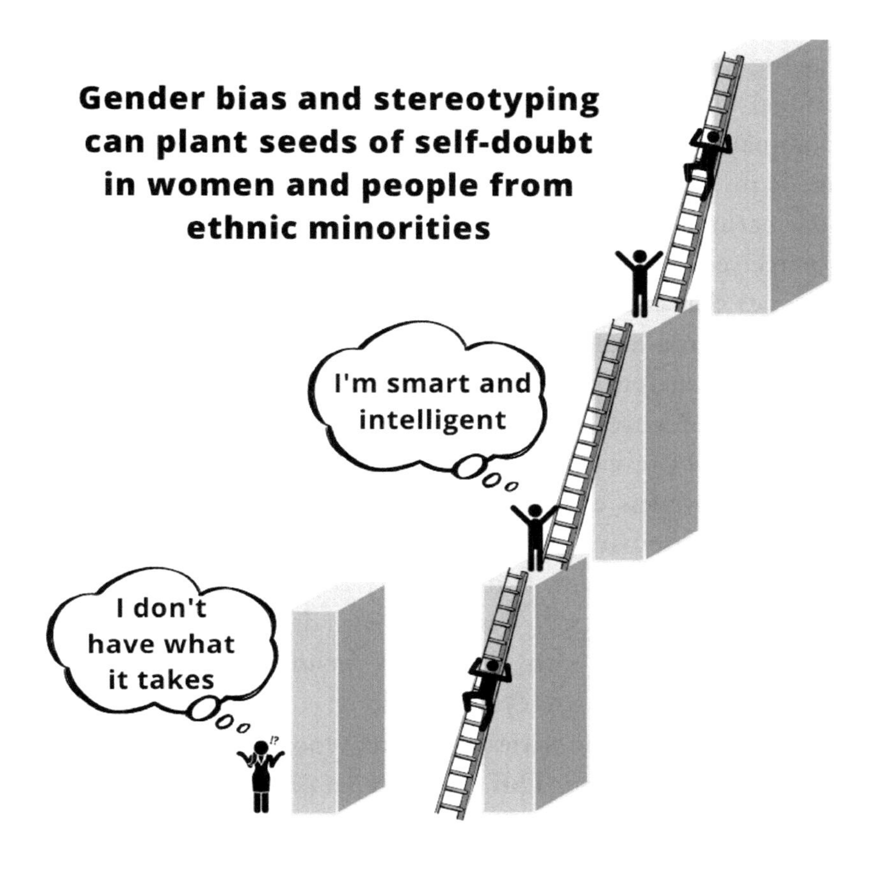

Here are the 3 common causes why imposter syndrome has an outsized effect on women and ethnic minorities:

1. Biases
2. Lack of representation
3. Microaggressions

Biases

Biases impact people's attitudes and behaviors in not only how they look at themselves, but also how they treat others. Common messaging that women are not good leaders because they're too emotional combined with the stereotype of a good leader with predominantly masculine traits—rational, agentic, assertive, and someone in complete control of their emotions—portrays men to be a more natural fit for leadership positions leaving women out who are perceived to be communal and warm. It's these gender stereotypes that can cause women to feel insecure, out of place, and not fit to be in a leadership position if she does make it to the top. Stereotypes such as this not only deprive us of female leaders but also deprive us of effective leaders.

Many studies reveal biases in the workplace based on the notion that women are less competent than men—they are paid less than their male counterparts for doing the same job, receive less support from senior management, and are more frequently passed over for important assignments.[11] For women, discrimination in the workplace combined with their own feelings of self-doubt can reinforce their belief that they don't belong.

Similarly, ethnic minorities are stereotyped to be unintelligent, lazy, and underachieving. This can cause an ethnic minority student to think that their admission to a prestigious university is the outcome of luck as opposed to something they actually deserve.

Lack of representation

Women and people from ethnic minorities are deemed fit for certain jobs and positions while considered unsuitable for others. This skews their representation in favor of certain professions—under-represented in surgery, over-represented in nursing; under-represented in technology, over-represented in HR; under-represented in leadership positions, over-represented at more junior levels.[12]

Lack of physical representation and proper role models in certain professions and positions can contribute to imposter syndrome.

When you don't see many examples of successful people who look like you and share your background, it's easy to assume that this success isn't meant for you. Being the only one who doesn't share an identity with others in the room can hit your confidence making you constantly doubt whether you're fit to be in this position.

Microaggressions

Our everyday interactions in how we are treated by others give us important social cues conveying whether others find us worthy thereby influencing how we see ourselves and if we consider fit to be a part of a certain group. Microaggressions are subtle, often unintentional behaviors that affect members of marginalized groups, and hit at the same doubts and feelings of self-worth that drive imposter syndrome.

Women and people from ethnic minorities are perceived and treated differently when they are:

- Less often sought out for advice.
- Excluded from important work-related discussions.
- Subjected to indirect put-downs, belittling, or bullying behavior.
- Mistaken for being at a lower job level than they really are.
- Consistently subjected to questioning in their area of expertise.
- Indirectly insulted through offensive and disrespectful remarks e.g. Being reassured that they are not like the negative stereotype of their marginalized group.
- Expected to follow a different set of rules for communication e.g. Judging a woman as harsh when she speaks with authority despite the same behavior being encouraged when it comes to her male counterparts.

Consistently subjected to doubt about their skills and status communicates that their ideas, knowledge, and insights are less valuable than others which in turn impacts their self-confidence and how effective they see themselves at work.

You can't get rid of stereotypes. At least not all by yourself. The best you can do is to acknowledge they exist and use them as input to determine if these stereotypes apply to you and whether they play a role in reinforcing your negative beliefs—subjecting you to deny your accomplishments, doubt your abilities, and feel less competent and capable.

Next time you find yourself thinking "I'm not smart enough and they are soon going to find out," take a moment to pause, look outside yourself and consider how your upbringing, organizational culture or negative stereotyping could be feeding those feelings of self-doubt. Once you are willing to accept that your beliefs are just a snapshot of your experiences and not a true measure of reality, you can be more open to exploring alternative views about yourself and better prepared to move ahead despite feeling those feelings.

Trish Taylor, author of *Yes! You Are Good Enough* says "Discover Your Origin Story. Our beliefs come from somewhere. We are not born believing that we are not good enough. Discovering where our beliefs came from is a good start. For some of us, it might be obvious. When you recognize negative stories coming from your own thoughts or even said out loud, take a moment to deconstruct them."[13]

Let's do this exercise to deconstruct your imposter origin story. The exercise is divided into two parts to help you look back at all the three different factors (childhood, organization culture, and stereotypes) that might be contributing to your imposter experience.

Exercise: What's Your Imposter Origin Story?

To identify your imposter origin story, read the questions in each of the sections below and write down your responses. Once you have completed the exercise, take time to highlight key messages, experiences, or events from your life that have impacted your confidence, sense of self-worth, understanding of intelligence, or the importance of success in significant ways. Taken together, they will give you useful inputs to construct your own imposter origin story.

Section 1: Messages in childhood

1. What messages did you receive as a child regarding your intelligence, skills, and abilities and how did these messages influence your behavior?
2. As a child, when you did something well or achieved success of any kind, how were you treated by your parents and other significant adults in your life—praised and inspired for doing well or ignored and discouraged to not talk about your accomplishments? What was your response—excited with a feeling of achievement or worried about how you could have done even better? How have these experiences impacted how you think about success today?
3. How did you respond to mistakes and failures as a child? How did you feel in those moments—embarrassed and disappointed or encouraged to try one more time? How did your parents and other significant adults in your life react to these difficulties—punish and ignore or inspire and encourage you to do better next time? How have these experiences shaped how you respond to mistakes and failures now?

4. How was success defined in your family? What were the academic and other expectations from you in terms of achievement? What does your family think about your current level of success now? How have the views of your parents and other significant adults in your life impacted how you think about success today?
5. As a girl child or a person from an ethnic minority (answer only if this applies to you), what were you told about what you can and can't do? Were you discouraged from trying certain things with the perception that you can never be good at them? What specific events or experiences made you feel that you don't belong?

Section 2: Impact of organization culture

1. How are you treated at work by your peers, managers, and leaders in the organization?
2. How would you describe the culture of your organization—empowering with a focus on learning or submissive with a focus on outcomes?
3. Do you feel safe to make mistakes, take risks and learn from your failures, or are you looked down upon when you do something wrong?
4. Are you inspired to achieve excellence or criticized for not meeting unrealistic goals or unhealthy levels of perfection?
5. Do you enjoy working with your team members and other coworkers or are you made to compete against them?
6. Do people at work respect boundaries between work and home or are you expected to be on all the time?
7. If you are a woman or a person from an ethnic minority, how are you made to feel by your peers, boss, and leaders in the organization? Do you feel supported or discriminated? Are

your ideas heard or ignored? Are there specific biases that prevent you from giving your best at work?
8. How do you feel (emotionally, mentally, and physically) about your work experience?

After thinking through the questions above, write down your imposter origin story.

Describe your imposter origin story

____

____

You can download a printable version of "What's Your Imposter Origin Story?" at:
techtello.com/rethink-imposter-syndrome/worksheets/

This exercise is bound to bring in some memories that may not be pleasant. You may feel disappointed, discouraged, or emotional right now. That's ok. Take this advice from Michelle Obama and own your story "Even when it's not pretty or perfect, even when it's more real than you want it to be, your story is what you have, what you will always have. It is something to own." Irrespective of what you have been told in the past, how you have been judged or criticized, or whatever biases you have had to face, remember this: you can't blame yourself for your environment and the people in it whose notions have had a big impact on the decisions you made and the way you lead your life. But you can take things under your control now and not let someone else's opinion become your reality. It's never too late to change your beliefs that can empower you instead of holding you back.

Self-awareness is the first step to do anything with clarity and intention. You've taken that one step out the door. You have shown the courage to own your imposter story. This in itself is no small feat. Take a moment to congratulate yourself. Feel good about coming this far because most people would much rather choose comfort and fear over courage and growth. As you take the next step on this journey of self-discovery, it's important to stay away from advice that does more damage than good. Prepare yourself to read all the advice in the next chapter and promise yourself to never apply the quick fixes and other harmful advice.

Chapter Summary

- Your personality may have a role to play if you have a tendency to focus on the negative and not the positive aspects of your life, but many factors outside of you also play a critical role in planting those seeds of self-doubt.
- Understanding your personal history—your upbringing, experiences growing up as a child, work culture, social interactions, and biases—is useful to identify when your feelings of not being good enough begin and what factors contributed to those limiting beliefs about yourself.
- Your negative beliefs about your sense of self-worth, capability, and competence are rooted in the messages you have been passed on as a child, inherent biases you face at work, and other stereotyped behaviors from people around you.

- The way you have been brought up to think about success, failure, and mistakes significantly impacts the way you think about them now. If your parents or other significant adults in your life thought less of you, conveyed that their love and approval were conditional on your performance, or refused to praise you for your good work, those experiences can make it hard for you to own your accomplishments and can later manifest as feelings of ineptness and self-doubt.
- The culture of your organization can either foster your growth or feed your insecurities. A toxic work culture can instill a sense of phoniness in you which stays with you throughout life.
- If you are a woman or a person from an ethnic minority, you might also be subjected to biases, microaggressions and other forms of prejudicial behaviors that make you think less about yourself and also what you can achieve. You may give up certain jobs and positions that are stereotyped to be not suitable for you or feel like you don't belong if you do end up in them.

Part 2

Impact of Imposter Syndrome

CHAPTER 6

Advice That Makes It Worse

THERE's A WEALTH of information on managing and getting past imposter syndrome. Just do a Google search and more than 5 million results will vie for your attention. Too much advice makes it hard to separate effective strategies that focus on long-term improvement from coping strategies that are workarounds to get over the temporary discomfort in the short term. Most dangerous are the quick-and-easy fixes and helpful tips: any advice tailored around building confidence by ignoring your feelings of self-doubt doesn't work. Even if you learn to suppress your low self-esteem and show confidence in certain situations, fixing the symptom without addressing the root cause only makes things worse. Your imposter experience stays with you. It keeps lurking around the corner waiting for the next opportunity to make you feel discouraged and declare you're incompetent.

When you take the right steps to manage your imposter feelings, it may seem like hard work at first. But, doing them right is the only way to make your effort stick and last long. For example...

- Appearing confident while giving a presentation is different from feeling worthy to give it. Worthiness comes first and then you practice appearing confident.
- Building the courage to speak up at work is different from believing that your ideas deserve to be heard. Acknowledging that you have something valuable to share comes first and then you build the courage to say it.
- Taking up an opportunity to appear capable is different from believing in your ability to make things work. Recognizing your unique talents and skills comes first and then it makes sense to go after the right opportunities.

Don't go after the band-aid solutions. They will only cover up your feelings briefly by making you feel better for a moment, a day, or perhaps even a week, while leaving you exposed once the effect of those band-aid solutions wanes.

As important as it is to apply the right strategies to manage your imposter syndrome, equally important is to know what constitutes bad advice. Knowing what isn't helpful will not only save you time, it will prevent you from applying advice that can amplify your feelings of uncertainty and self-doubt.

Four most common pieces of advice for imposter syndrome to avoid at all costs:

1. It's you
2. Fake it till you make it
3. Try positive thinking
4. Just push on through

It's you

When Pauline Rose and Suzanne Imes first identified the imposter phenomenon in 1978, they theorized that women were uniquely affected by imposter syndrome. Since then, research has shown that imposter syndrome isn't limited to women and both men and women experience imposter feelings.[1] Even though feelings of self-doubt, uncertainty, and inadequacy associated with imposter syndrome affect all kinds of people, most discussions about imposter syndrome continue to focus on women.

In fact, one study that explored how men and women react to performance conditions (feedback and accountability), identified that men are more likely to experience the imposter phenomenon when given negative feedback regarding their performance.[2] The study concluded with three major findings:

- Men experience higher state stress than women when given negative feedback.
- Men decrease their effort and perform worse than women under conditions of high accountability.
- Women increase their effort and display higher performance when given negative feedback.

Men don't report feelings of inadequacy and uncertainty about their skills and abilities while women talk about it all the time, not because of the absence of imposter syndrome in men. It's the cultural gender norms that tell men to suck it up and get going to avoid appearing vulnerable.

This leads to two issues:

1. Women who have healthy feelings of self-doubt are made to believe they have imposter syndrome.

2. Men who actually have imposter syndrome fail to acknowledge it and adopt unhealthy practices to deal with their feelings of ineptness.

Any advice that targets your imposter feelings because you're a female and suggests that you can't have those feelings if you are a male isn't backed by science. Ignore it and move on.

Fake it till you make it

The most common advice you will hear to deal with feelings of inadequacy is to "fake it till you make it."

Fake your confidence.
Fake your competence.
Fake your motivation.

There's no shortage of fake it 'til you make it advice. Amy Cuddy, a social psychologist, and an author popularized the idea further in her famous TED talk in which she said "Don't fake it 'til you make it. Fake it 'til you become it."[3]

Faking it by posturing, pretending to be confident, and ignoring those nagging doubts can offer some temporary respite from those feelings of self-doubt, but once you're done putting on a show, being inauthentic to yourself negatively impacts your perceptions of yourself. Imitating confidence and competency has long-term implications.

This is what happened with Laura Huang, a professor of business administration at Harvard Business School. In college, when Laura was dealing with feelings of uncertainty and self-doubt, she turned to the most popular advice "fake it till you make it"—pretend to be confident and act the part even though you're secretly nervous and your inner monologue is screaming and telling you're a fake.

Laura was one of the four females majoring in electrical engineering and had a fear of being stereotyped. So, she tried to act the part of the masculine persona typical of engineering majors "I postured and pretended, but no matter what amount of faking it I put out, I found myself with more self-doubt than when I started."[4] After college, in her role at a new company, she tried faking it again. This time she took advice from a friend who suggested her to act with the confidence of a white male, but her attempt to fake it backfired "I got pushback. People saw me as aggressive. I felt superficial, came across as inauthentic and wasn't getting the sort of support or social acceptance that my elite brass male peers were." Laura later noted that faking it by being inauthentic did not help her. Rather, it negatively affected her performance in the long term.

Consider for yourself.

Let's say you just finished a big project and your team congratulates you for doing a terrific job. What would be your reaction if you believe that you just faked your way through it? Won't you discredit all the hard work you put into making things happen, deny your accomplishment and feel like a complete fraud? By identifying yourself as a fake in the "fake it till you make it" advice, you inadvertently end up calling yourself a fraud—someone who actually isn't competent and was just putting on a show.

In trying to cope with your feelings of inadequacy, consciously choosing to behave in a way that is fake reinforces the belief that you're indeed a fake. "Fake it till you make it" compounds feelings of imposter syndrome because saying that you were just faking it makes you internalize those negative beliefs about yourself. Sort of a self-fulfilling prophecy.

Alan Ibbotson, founder and coach says that we should bury the phrase completely "It literally means you can't do it or be it, and you are pretending. For some, they are signing up to be a fake and a phony, a liar and a cheat, someone who isn't concerned with what others think or even with being authentic in their success — they just want to get away with it, operating on the hope that eventually they'll make it."[5]

Managing your imposter feelings isn't about faking competence in areas you aren't good at; it requires recognizing your true skills and abilities. Next time you aren't so sure about yourself and someone tells you to "just fake it," tell them you would much rather stay authentic, build genuine confidence and see how it goes.

Try positive thinking

When you're struggling with imposter feelings, another common piece of advice says repeating positive phrases to yourself can change your life, encouraging some version of:

I am successful.
I am confident and competent.
I am not a fraud.

No doubt, being optimistic and staying positive can be incredibly powerful. But thinking positive thoughts only helps when it does not minimize or invalidate how you really feel about yourself. When what you say consciously does not align with how you think about yourself subconsciously, you can't expect your subconscious part of the brain to sit quiet. It shouts back drifting your mind to the same old thoughts planted deep in your brain through months and sometimes years of rehearsing the negative self-talk "I'm not good enough. I don't have the competence. They're soon going to find out."

For example:

- If you say to yourself "I will succeed," while deep down you believe that you're not worthy of success, your subconscious mind is going to fight back "You aren't worthy and you know it. Don't fool yourself."
- If you say to yourself "I'm competent," while you have the habit of constantly doubting your skills and abilities, your subconscious mind will remind you "Remember all the mistakes you have made at work and all the failures you have had to face."
- If you say to yourself "I'm not a fraud," while feeling like a fraud is something you've identified with yourself for a very long time, your subconscious mind will tell you "How can you forget about all the times you succeeded because of luck?"

Thinking positive thoughts by themselves does not work when you use them to suppress your feelings of inadequacy or avoid dealing with negative emotions. Telling yourself to "stop thinking about them" or "ignore them and get going" backfires—your negative emotions don't leave you alone. Rather trying to avoid them makes them emerge much stronger later.

You don't need positive thinking. What you need are strategies to reframe your negative self-talk. Strategies that will empower you to shift from self-defeating behaviors to constructive action. Strategies that will make your self-talk work for you and not against you. We will learn about these reframing techniques in the later chapters.

Just push on through

When others find you capable and intelligent and really don't understand what you're going through, they might suggest this:

> Quit stressing.
> Get over it.
> Just push on through.

The real problem isn't taking action despite feeling fearful. If you keep waiting for a perfect moment when you won't fear the thing, you might have to wait a very long time. It's pushing on through while ignoring your feelings of self-doubt, uncertainty, and inadequacy that makes it worse.

Darren Ryan learned this the hard way. He experienced imposter syndrome at different points in his career, but his feelings of being a fraud intensified when he became CEO of Social Entrepreneurs Ireland at the age of 29.[6] Despite being committed to the organization and feeling passionate about the impact he could make, Ryan was terrified of messing it all up and constantly doubted himself.

At first, when he felt like an imposter, he ignored those thoughts and focused on people around him who believed in him. He disregarded his imposter feelings, gave himself a pep talk, and kept going despite feeling fearful. It didn't work. Those nagging feelings of self-doubt kept coming back, putting intense pressure on him to do something that he thought he could never possibly achieve. Luckily, Ryan realized that ignoring his feelings wasn't the solution. To move forward, he needed to embrace how he felt.

What happens though when unlike Darren you refuse to acknowledge your imposter feelings and keep burying, ignoring, and denying them? Working hard to cover them up and forcing yourself to take action can lead to negative ruminations with devastating consequences:

- Mental health issues like anxiety and depression.[7]
- Harmful coping strategies like alcohol or other substance abuse to cope with the stress.[8]
- Feeling of isolation by never letting anyone into what you're worried about.
- Exhaustion and job burnout from living with a constant fear of discovery.
- Increased feelings of guilt, shame, worthlessness, or hopelessness.
- Limiting professional growth by intentionally passing up opportunities, or quitting before accomplishing your goals.[9]

When you find yourself consumed by imposter feelings, don't apply the "quit stressing" and "get going" advice. Rather, sit with the discomfort, and acknowledge how you're feeling first. Embracing your imposter feelings will not make them go away, but letting them in is the only way to make space for the good things in your life.

Don't settle. Don't look for shortcuts or quick wins. Don't go after the fake it till you make it, positive thinking and pushing on through advice. They may give you temporary relief from the burden of your negative thoughts, but becoming addicted to those short-term fixes will make you blind to the long-term impact they have on your life. Things won't be that hard once you learn to get over your imposter feelings. And you know what's the best part: you'll finally get to see what others see in you—a confident and capable person who knows their strengths but recognizes their limits too. Someone who's not ready to give up without trying. Someone who's willing to take the risk because they care more about learning and less about proving themselves right. Because in the end what matters is not how others see you, but how you see yourself through your own eyes.

Think about that person you wish to become. What gaps do you see from where you are to where you want to be? What stands in its way? Yes, it's your self-limiting beliefs about your competence and worth, but that's just part of the story. When you feel like you don't belong, when you struggle to feel competent, and when you constantly doubt your achievements, it impacts not only your thinking but also your actions. In the next chapter, you'll identify self-sabotage behaviors and the five coping mechanisms that you may adopt to deal with your imposter feelings.

Chapter Summary

- What's worse than feeling like a fake? Finding fake advice. The popularity of this psychological pattern has spawned many self-proclaimed gurus with advice to fix you—20 simple tips to overcome imposter syndrome, 9 easy ways to deal with imposter syndrome, 10 quick steps you can use to overcome imposter syndrome. It's these quick and easy fixes that are fake and not you.
- Shifting from seeing yourself as a fraud to a person with genuine abilities requires hard work. Temporary fixes may offer some respite from your stress and anxiety, but not for long.
- Research has refuted all claims that put the burden of imposter experience on women. Men are as likely to feel it. Despite science to back it up, women continue to be targeted for their feelings of inadequacy. Any advice that tells women

"it's you" and men to believe "it's not for you" is misguided. Ignore it.

- "Fake it till you make it" is one of the most popular pieces of advice on faking your way to success. But think about it for a moment. If you're already feeling like a fraud, how can signing up to fake your confidence, fake your skills, or whatever other faking you need to do be any good for you? It only reinforces your doubts about not being competent and good enough.
- No doubt ruminating on negative emotions is unhelpful. But simply repeating positive phrases to yourself won't make your insecurities disappear either. Positive thinking does not work when used to suppress negative emotions. Instead, mentally empower yourself by reframing negative self-talk from destructive behaviors to constructive action.
- Pushing on through is a great strategy for taking action. But not so much when you deny your imposter feelings. Forcing yourself to take action while trying hard to cover up your negative emotions leads to self-sabotage behaviors that impact your mental health and personal well-being.

CHAPTER 7

Coping Behaviors That Keep You Stuck

HOW DO YOU behave when a voice yelling you're an imposter rings loudly in your head? You may acknowledge your negative thoughts, but do you also acknowledge your defeatist behavior? When most people share their imposter experience, all they do is talk about the "voice" while disregarding the underlying behaviors they picked up consciously or unconsciously as coping mechanisms to deal with that voice—destructive behaviors with unrealistic notions of what it means to be competent or that sets the internal bar so high that it seems almost impossible to achieve. Behaviors that make them drag their feet. Behaviors that are not only damaging to their own growth but hurt those around them as well.

Think about that voice in your head. How does it make you behave?

- What do you do when you come across something difficult to do?
- What's your reaction to mistakes?
- Do you play safe or do you put yourself out there and risk being judged?

- Do you go with unpopular opinions or do things that will make others admire you?
- Do you put things off with a fear of failure?

As a human being, you are wired to react to the events around you. Events impact your emotions, emotions shape your experience and your experience finally affects your behavior. So, an event that makes you feel confident, powerful, and in control will trigger a different behavior than if you were anxious, fearful, or stressed. Ideally, a positive event should trigger a positive emotion leading to positive behavior while a negative event should trigger a negative emotion with negative behavior. But not for people with imposter syndrome. For them, even a positive event like a promotion or an opportunity to handle higher-level responsibilities can lead to negative feelings of low self-worth and inadequacy.

So, if it's not the event that triggers a specific behavior, what does? It's your belief. When you carry a story with you that is not empowering, you can adopt dysfunctional behaviors to deal with feelings of inadequacy, or as Emma Gannon, author and podcaster puts it "We can become obsessed with our own thoughts. We can tell ourselves we can't do it. We can make up endless excuses for years. We can give up right before we reach the finish line. We can bottle it before a big work event. There is often a saboteur living in our mind and it tells us believable, perfectly packaged lies and can ruin everything if we aren't careful. When I think of sabotage in day-to-day life, the main theme is believing I am not worthy of a great life. Naively, I thought that my imposter syndrome would disappear when I became more experienced or successful on paper. Turns out that proven success is where sabotage thrives. The less of an imposter I become, the more I feel like one."[1]

Self-sabotage from imposter syndrome can show up in many strange ways and it plays out differently with each one of us. For example...

- Your inner dialogue may tell you to keep quiet and not voice your opinion unless you are 100% confident about its correctness. Worried that a less than perfect answer will expose you.
- When you need help, your inner critic might stop you. What if asking for help makes you look incompetent and conveys to others that you don't deserve this position?
- You may stay back late and work extra hard. Your negative sense of self-worth makes you overwork in order to keep up with all the intelligent and smart people around you.
- You keep putting off an important assignment with the worry that you'll screw it up. It's much easier to not try than to put yourself through the humiliation of coming up short.
- You may have big ideas but never see them through. It feels safe because when you don't finish the project others can never judge you.

Judy Ho, a forensic neuropsychologist and tenured Associate Professor of Psychology at Pepperdine University says "The source of self-sabotage is part of a common ancestral and evolutionary adaptation that has allowed us to persevere as a species in the first place. We are essentially programmed to strive for goals because achieving them makes us feel good. That dopamine rush is an incentive to repeat those behaviors. The trick, especially when it comes to self-sabotage, is that our biochemistry doesn't necessarily discriminate between the kind of feel-good sensations we experience when we are going toward our goals and the 'good' feelings we get when we avoid something that seems threatening."[2]

In other words, you are more likely to self-sabotage when your desire to avoid threats is higher than your need to achieve. Feelings of fraudulence can create a fear of discovery so high that it can make you adopt destructive coping mechanisms to deal with your feelings of inadequacy.

PERPETUATING IMPOSTER SYNDROME

Your imposter feelings may not be with you all the time, but the way you behave when those feelings strike gives them permission to stick around. The more you do it, the more powerful they become. The more you latch onto these behaviors, the more they turn into a trap.

- When you beat yourself up for making a mistake, it reinforces the belief "you don't have what it takes."
- When you work extra hard to look competent like others, it reinforces the belief "you don't have the skills."
- When you keep delaying a project for fear of failure, it reinforces the belief "you'll never succeed."
- When you avoid an opportunity for fear of discovery, it reinforces the belief "it's better to play safe."

Feeling you're not good enough, doubting your competence, questioning your skills and abilities happens in your head. But what you do with them shows up in your actions. Your behavior may look like a shield to protect you from feeling bad about yourself, but all it does is expose you to more negative feelings and hurt emotions. You may keep going down a rabbit hole unless you learn to identify patterns of behavior that perpetuate your imposter feelings and hold you back.

This is what happened with Georgina Lawton, an author, and journalist who adopted self-sabotage behaviors when she felt undeserving of success: "Handing things in late always fills me with insurmountable fear and self-loathing—but I do it all the time. I piss my plans up the wall and wreck my well-thought-out ideas on a near-daily basis; I knock back tequilas when a deadline is looming, I blank important emails, I test the strength of my relationships, and shrug sleep away at 3am when I know I have to do something that scares me the next day. If everyone abandons me, if I get fired, if I miss my meeting, then it proves what I suspected all along: that I am totally inadequate."[3]

Brandi Carlile, a singer, and songwriter who earned 18 Grammy Award nominations spoke about the self-sabotage behaviors she adopted to deal with her feelings of inadequacy "If I didn't say yes to everything, eventually everyone was going to find out how unqualified I am to be in the position I'm in. I'm going to stop getting invited, and I'm going back to the bars if I don't show up for everybody's thing. I was getting really tired and empty. I was not headed for a good outcome, I was about to crash and burn. I was headed back into destruction for sure, and didn't see it coming."[4]

What about you? What behaviors do you pick up consciously or unconsciously as coping mechanisms to deal with your imposter feelings? Let's find out. Your imposter experience can manifest in the following ways:

1. Procrastinator
2. Perfectionist
3. Overworker
4. People Pleaser
5. Self-Diminisher

Procrastinator

You're a procrastinator if you have the tendency to put things off or delay them till the very last moment. You can give excuses all you want "I am not able to find time" "I work well under pressure," but the real reason to avoid the very thing you need to do isn't lack of time or your ability to produce great work under a time crunch. It's your fear of doing a bad job, making it evident to yourself and others that you're actually a fraud.

Your imposter feelings can make you procrastinate when you hold these beliefs:

- Any mistakes or failures signal I am bad and worthless.
- I am not competent if I don't perform exceptionally well.
- What I consider as my best effort can never be good enough.

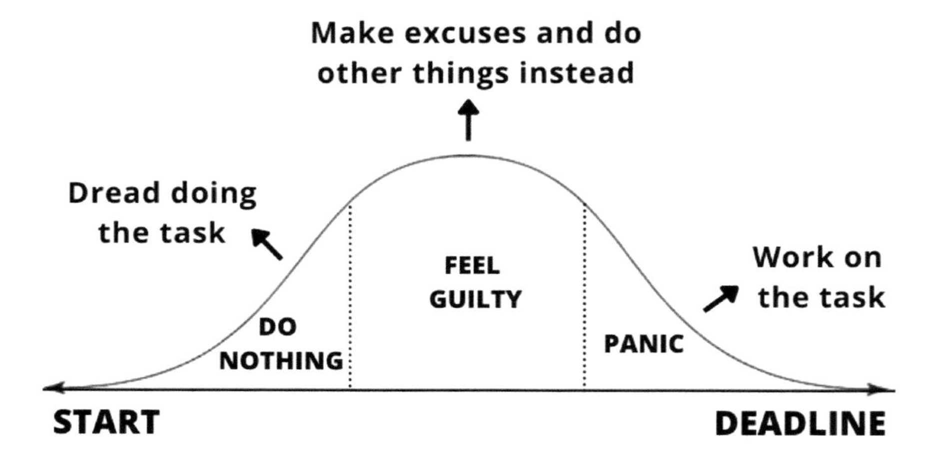

At times, we all procrastinate. But if you are dealing with feelings of imposter syndrome, procrastination isn't a one-off thing. It's more like a habit. And every time you behave this way and still end up getting a good outcome, the unexpected success only intensifies your imposter feelings and reinforces your beliefs that your success is due to luck and not your abilities. After all, you didn't put in the effort and don't deserve this outcome. You may have fooled everyone again, but not for long. And if the outcome of your procrastination doesn't turn out well, you can give yourself an excuse that you could have done better had you spent more time.

To understand how this plays out, imagine that your boss asks you to put together a proposal for a new product that's due in two weeks. There are two possibilities:

Get to work right away: You work hard during these two weeks and put together a great proposal for the product. However, your boss doesn't like it. In this case, your best effort turns out to be not good enough. If you already deal with feelings of fraudulence, it can leave you questioning yourself, your competence, and your ability. Receiving criticism can expose you to others and invoke feelings of shame and humiliation.

Procrastinate: You avoid working on the proposal till the last day. With only a day to meet the deadline, you work throughout the day and night to get it ready in time for review. A bad outcome won't be a surprise—you could have done better had you spent more time. A good outcome serves as evidence you're not worthy—you didn't work hard and just got lucky this time.

While doing the work exposes you to criticism, procrastination insulates you from the mortifying feeling that your best effort may not be good enough. Many people with imposter feelings opt for procrastination because they don't consciously make the right choice. They fail to ask:

1. What is it that I am trying to avoid?
2. What's my real reason for putting it off?
3. What's the worst that can happen if I give it my best shot?
4. Why do I really care so much about what others think of me that I am willing to sabotage my own chance of success?

Perfectionist

You're a perfectionist if you have a long list of what constitutes wrong, but only one way of it being right—your way. Exemplary performance, high standards, and 100% perfect outcome just the way you expect. Things have to be your way or they are simply not "good enough." You set excessively high, unrealistic goals and then experience self-defeating thoughts and behaviors when you don't reach those goals.

Your imposter feelings turn you into a perfectionist when you:

- Feel obligated to overdeliver.
- Have a strong tendency to classify everything as important.
- Known to push your limits or always strive for more.
- Have a tendency to obsess over minute details even when they don't add value.
- Rarely satisfied with your achievements because you believe you could have done even better.
- Set extremely high standards for yourself and others that are almost impossible to achieve.
- Anything short of a flawless performance leaves you feeling unsatisfied.

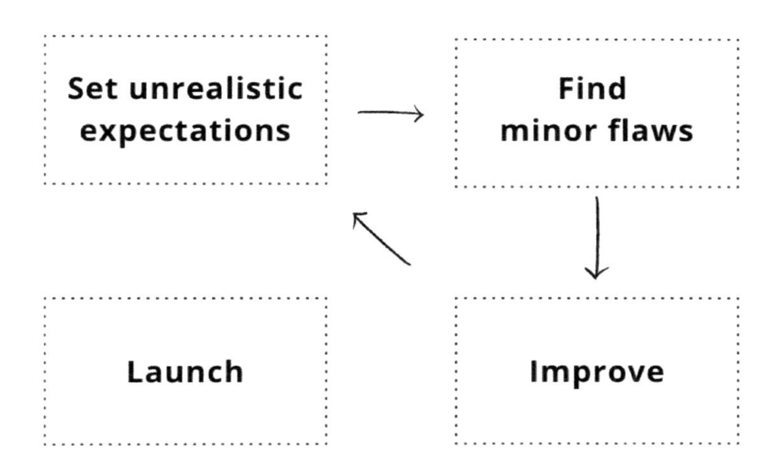

Julia Cameron, author of *The Artist's Way* writes "Perfectionism has nothing to do with getting it right. It has nothing to do with having high standards. Perfectionism is a refusal to let yourself move ahead...Perfectionism is not a quest for the best. It is a pursuit of the worst in ourselves, the part that tells us that nothing we do will ever be good enough—that we should try again."[5]

Your perfectionist attitude impacts how you collaborate with others. Not only do you have great difficulty delegating—even if you're able to do so—your inner perfectionist is never satisfied, often left feeling angry, frustrated, and dissatisfied. Pushing others to meet your high standards can turn you into a control freak. It can convey a lack of trust making others avoid you or when left without a choice they may show resistance to put in their best effort and do genuinely good work. There's a fine line between healthy striving and setting goals that make you and others miserable. The drive to excel is not the same as the drive to perfect. They are two very different things. Excellence is about utilizing your and others' potential to seek a great outcome. Perfectionism is about obsession to the point of being self-destructive.

When failure and rejection seem debilitating, it definitely feels safer to keep tweaking and editing. However, in doing so, you fail to get the feedback and learning lessons that are crucial for your growth. Your quest for perfection doesn't make things better, it only brings a whole lot of misery. Brené Brown, a research professor, and author calls perfectionism "the 20-ton shield."[6] She says "We carry it around, thinking it's going to protect us from being hurt. But it protects us from being seen." Setting excessively high goals for yourself and failing to achieve them confirms your fears: you're simply not good enough and irrespective of how hard you try, you may never measure up.

Many people with imposter feelings give in to their perfectionist tendencies because they don't consciously make the right choice. They fail to ask:

1. What makes me believe this is important?
2. Does my opinion match with what others have to say? What's their reason for agreement or disagreement?
3. What will be the impact of not making this change? What's the absolute worst that can happen?
4. What other things can I do in its place that will bring more value to me, my team, and my organization?

Overworker

You're an *overworker* if hard work, over-preparation, and long hours are your default strategies to avoid being intimidated by all the smart and intelligent people around you. You believe that the only reason you have come so far without being exposed is your ability to work harder than anyone else. And when all that anxiety, hard work, and suffering makes you do well, you discredit your success to effort which further spurs you to work harder than everyone else.

Your imposter feelings turn you into an *overworker* when you:

- Constantly work late and go beyond what's expected.
- Get stressed when you're not working.
- Addicted to the validation that comes from working.
- Have trouble switching off from work.
- Believe the only way to prove your worth is to work harder than everyone else.

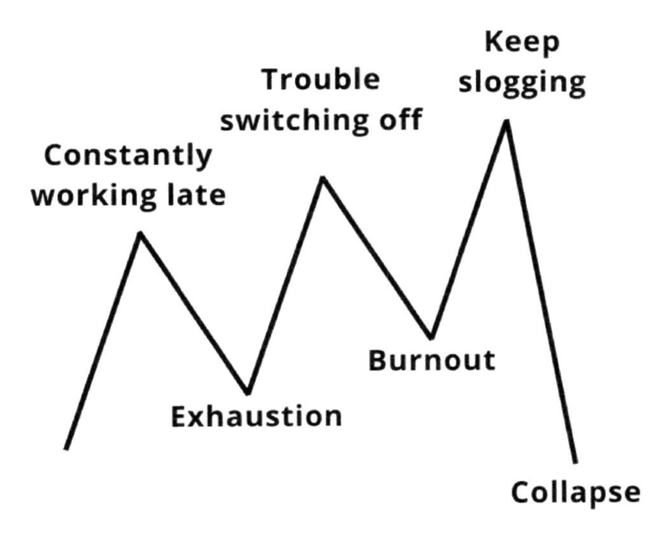

Arianna Huffington, co-founder of The Huffington Post and the founder of Thrive Global who collapsed from sleep deprivation and exhaustion, broke her cheekbone, and woke up in a pool of blood writes about her wake-up call in her book *Thrive* "We think, mistakenly, that success is the result of the amount of time we put in at work, instead of the quality of time we put in."[7] When you're dealing with feelings of fraudulence you don't think this way: all those extra hours not only seem necessary, they become an essential part of your existence. Putting in the effort isn't about doing a good job, it's about saving yourself from falling short. Achieving success isn't about celebrating your accomplishments, it's about hiding your shortcomings.

Coping up with the voice in your head that keeps telling you "you're not who everyone thinks you are" adds to your struggles. This never-ending cycle of the feeling of ineptness, hard work, and success, followed by more ineptness is only a trap. Before you know it, it turns you into a workaholic. It keeps you on your toes with the belief that the only way to cover up your fraud is to work harder than everyone else. Working super hard may temporarily combat your feelings of imposter syndrome, but the price you have to pay is significantly higher. Spending all that time working makes you neglect your health leading to exhaustion and burnout. You may also spend less time with your family. Is your professional success really worth all this sacrifice?

Many people with imposter feelings overwork because they don't consciously make the right choice. They fail to ask:

1. What's my reason for putting in these extra hours?
2. What will these extra hours help me earn? Why are they more important than other things in my life?
3. What do these extra hours help me avoid? Why am I right in avoiding those things?

4. Instead of working hard to prove my competence to others, what if I focus on becoming my best self?

People Pleaser

You're a people pleaser if your actions stem from your desire to convince others to like you. You desperately seek their approval and acceptance not because you trust their judgment, but as a measure to fool them into believing you're worthy and that you belong. You think that others are less likely to find out that you are an imposter if they like you.

Your imposter feelings turn you into a people pleaser when you:

- Constantly seek approval and acceptance.
- Fearful of saying no.
- Act out of fear of being rejected and disliked.
- Push your personal commitments aside to make time for others.
- Have a hard time delegating work or letting others down.
- Feel angry and resentful in trying to meet others' expectations.
- Feel exhausted from pretending and trying to keep everyone happy.
- Prioritize helping others at the cost of your own health.
- Make decisions based on others' sense of right and wrong as opposed to standing up to what's right.

Aziz Gazipura, author of *Not Nice* writes "At its core, being nice is about being liked by others by making everything smooth. No waves, no friction. It's based on this (woefully inaccurate) theory: If I please others, give them everything they want, keep a low profile, and don't ruffle feathers or create any discomfort, then others will like me, love me, and shower me with approval and anything else I want."[8] However, turning to people-pleasing as a coping strategy is self-destructive—being inauthentic creates a conflict between your inner feelings and how you appear on the outside, which further intensifies your feelings of unworthiness and inadequacy.

Helping others out of genuine care goes a long way in establishing trust and building better relationships. But when it stems from the desire to make others think favorably of you, manipulating how they perceive you by doing things that make them happy, seeking constant validation, acceptance, and approval to establish your own sense of self-worth, it's utterly damaging to your relationship with others. You are not acting out of your sense of goodness for others but rather it's deeply seated in your fear of rejection, feeling of helplessness, risk of failure, discomfort from displeasing others, and not having the courage to receive their disapproval.

Many people with imposter feelings turn into people pleasers because they don't consciously make the right choice. They fail to ask:

1. What's driving my current behavior—fear of being rejected or a genuine desire to help?
2. Can I really build better relationships by fooling others to like me?
3. What's more important—seeking approval or adding value?

Self-Diminisher

You are a self-diminisher if you have the tendency to over-index on your mistakes without acknowledging all the good things you have done and achieved in your life. When you succeed or do something well, instead of congratulating yourself for doing a good job, you obsess about a minor thing that went wrong. This is how the dialogue goes on in your mind. "Every mistake reflects on my competence." "Every failure signals to others that I have cheated my way and I am completely undeserving of this position."

Your imposter feelings turn you into a self-diminisher when you:

- Try to play safe by sticking to things you know well.
- Over-index on mistakes and failures and try to avoid them at all costs.

- Give up on opportunities that require you to step outside your comfort zone.
- Avoid challenges because it's uncomfortable and risky to try something you're not good at.

IMPOSTER FEELINGS CAN TURN YOU INTO A SELF DIMINISHER

Staying within your comfort zone for feeling like a fraud can make you feel safe, but at what cost? Your behavior not only diminishes what you achieve but also makes you give up on opportunities that you're very well suited to perform. When not doing well evokes feelings of guilt and shame, it only makes you give up too soon. Unwilling to take risks limits your options. Avoiding challenges and setbacks can become your goal, but it also keeps success away from your reach. Without building the skills and abilities necessary to grow, you continue to find yourself ill-suited to perform which further intensifies your feelings of inadequacy.

Many people with imposter feelings diminish their own potential because they don't consciously make the right choice. They fail to ask:

1. What will staying within my comfort zone help me achieve?
2. How can I learn and grow if I never make mistakes?
3. What do my past failures and mistakes teach me?
4. What will the new opportunity help me learn?

Your beliefs about yourself and your self-worth can lead to these limiting behaviors—procrastinator, perfectionist, overworker, people pleaser, or self-diminisher. You may latch onto one of these behaviors more frequently than others and also use several of them in different contexts and situations. However, none of these behaviors protect you from imposter feelings. You may engage in them to get some respite from feeling like a fraud, but when repeated often, your brain takes over—it makes these decisions for you. You see this is the biggest problem: you may behave this way and not even realize. Unless you pause, take a moment to recognize them, and break free of these self-limiting behaviors, they will continue to feed your insecurities. Getting over your imposter feelings isn't just about building confidence: there's no magic pill to get over negative patterns of self-sabotage and self-doubt. It requires getting rid of behaviors that destroy that confidence.

Let's do this exercise to identify the self-sabotage behaviors and coping mechanisms you adopt to deal with your imposter feelings.

Exercise: What's Your Coping Strategy?

Think about achievement related tasks from the past that made you feel like an imposter, for example...

- Giving a presentation
- Working on a new assignment
- Interviewing for a job position
- Getting a promotion
- Negotiating a deal
- Acquiring a big client

Look at the self-sabotage behaviors described with each of the five coping mechanisms earlier (procrastinator, perfectionist, overworker, people pleaser, or self-diminisher). Which self-sabotage behaviors and coping mechanisms best describe how you deal with your achievement related situations? Write them down below.

My pre-dominant coping mechanisms are ____________________ and ____________________.

1. Describe your most recent experience demonstrating your pre-dominant coping mechanism.

    ____

    ____

2. What limiting beliefs about yourself made you adopt this behavior?

____

____

3. There's a pattern that triggers this behavior. Can you identify it?

____

____

You can download a printable version of "What's Your Coping Strategy?" at:
techtello.com/rethink-imposter-syndrome/worksheets/

The risk of facing criticism can make you procrastinate, desire for flawless execution can turn you into a perfectionist, relying solely on effort can turn you into a workaholic, using external validation as a measure of your worth can make you a people pleaser and the fear of unknowns can lead to diminishing potential. Knowing what triggers your insecurities and the coping mechanisms you adopt to deal with the anxiety of feeling like an imposter is a big step. It gives you an opportunity to understand the difference between behaviors that push you forward and the ones that pull you back. It creates an awareness that's essential to break free from your default tendency to try to save yourself and instead build the courage to reclaim your excellence.

So far you've only been concerned about yourself. Worried how your feelings might get in the way of making meaningful progress. But did you also consider the consequences of thinking this way on others? Your feelings of not being good enough do not end with you.

They have a very real impact on others. In the next chapter, you'll understand how your negative thinking can cause a domino effect across your organization. A crippling sense of failure, constantly doubting your competence, and feeding your insecurities with defensive behaviors can hurt your team's morale and destroy your company's performance.

Chapter Summary

- Your feeling of being a fraud isn't just limited to your thoughts. It feeds into your emotions, experiences and ultimately affects the way you act.
- What holds you back is not just your fear, but your attitude towards it. Lack of belief in your skills and abilities can make you self-sabotage by adopting destructive coping mechanisms to deal with your feelings of inadequacy. The tighter you hold onto these behaviors to avoid feeling bad about yourself, the more stuck you'll be.
- Your imposter feelings turn you into a procrastinator if you put important things off or delay them with the fear of producing a bad outcome. Having less time at hand to complete the task saves you from the shame and embarrassment of putting in your best effort and still not doing a good job.
- Worrying that anything less than perfect will signal incompetence to others and expose you as a fraud makes you a perfectionist. You obsess about minor details, constantly tweak without releasing, and refuse to receive feedback.

- When everyone around you seems smart and intelligent except you, you think your only option to hide your incompetence is by working extra hard. This limiting belief about your abilities turns you into a workaholic. Boundaries between work and home start to blur. In the long run, it leads to exhaustion and burnout.
- When others like you, it makes you feel safe from the danger of being exposed as a fraud. Doing things to make others happy can turn you into a people pleaser. You make decisions based on what others will like as opposed to what's the right thing to do.
- When you think every mistake and failure reflects on your competence, you try to play safe and give up on opportunities that require stepping outside your comfort zone. You would much rather diminish your own potential than risk fear of discovery.

CHAPTER 8

Cost to Others of Feeling Like a Fraud

THERANOS, FOUNDED by Elizabeth Holmes in 2003, a nineteen-year-old Stanford chemical and electrical engineering drop-out was a consumer healthcare technology startup that was once valued at $10 billion. The company claimed to revolutionize the blood-testing industry through its proprietary testing technology and a device that could run a multitude of tests on a patient's physiology within minutes and at a fraction of the cost of current technology. However, the technological breakthrough that CEO Elizabeth Holmes and former company president Ramesh Balwani touted was never demonstrated, and the assertions of Holmes and Balwani amounted to outright deceit. Holmes and Balwani were ultimately charged by the SEC for massive fraud. The company shut down operations in September 2018, laying off hundreds of its employees. Despite having an "all-star board," the company failed to find a buyer causing all equity investments in the company to be made worthless by the shutdown.[1]

In another story, WeWork, the real estate company, founded by Adam Neumann in 2010 which provides flexible shared workspaces for technology startups and services for other enterprises, filed documents for an initial public offering of shares in August 2019.

However, six weeks later, Neumann voted to remove himself from the CEO job and had given up his majority control of WeWork's stock. The company's proposed valuation fell from $47 billion to $10 billion, less than the $12.8 billion it had raised since 2010. The IPO was called off entirely.

What went wrong? Several factors led to its misfortunes: an expensive business model, self-dealing and self-enrichment behavior exhibited by Neumann. Neumann borrowed money from WeWork at little to no interest and privately bought properties which he then leased back to WeWork. So, the company paid him rent while also lending him money. Neumann's private jet trips involved incidental transportation of marijuana across international borders, and his wife Rebekah Neumann demanded that employees be fired after meeting them for mere minutes because she disliked their energy. That's not it. The company was sued several times for race and gender discrimination and sexual harassment. In 2019, almost 20% of its workforce globally was laid-off in an attempt to right-size the business.[2]

Elizabeth Holmes and Adam Neumann were the real frauds who not only cheated their investors of billions of dollars but also impacted the lives of thousands of people who lost their jobs during these debacles. You aren't a real imposter like Elizabeth Holmes or Adam Neumann.

You haven't cheated your way to the top. They did.
You're not making false promises. They did.
You're not pretending to be someone you're not. They did.

EFFECT OF IMPOSTER SYNDROME ON OTHERS

Constant self-doubt cascades negativity to others

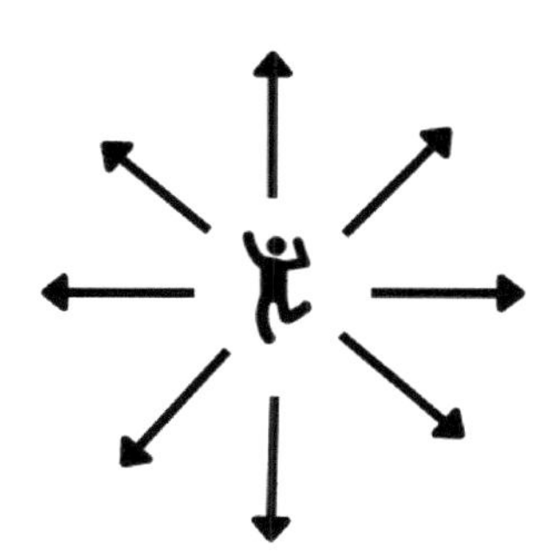

Confidence spreads positive vibes and uplifts people

You may not be a real imposter, but there are dangers of feeling like a fake. When fear of failure seems debilitating, when you don't consider mistakes as great opportunities for learning, and when you believe that you're just winging it and can be found out any minute, these feelings don't just stop with you. They are also damaging to others around you. In an organization, people working together are like dominos. One person's negativity can cause a chain reaction: a shift in other people's beliefs surrounding that person and cascade that negativity to the entire organization. Just like a line of dominos falling over, when one of the dominos falls, it triggers the next one, and the next...your imposter feelings can create a cascading domino effect which can hurt the performance of your entire organization.

DOMINO EFFECT

If you are a leader, manager, or someone in a position of power who can influence other people or play a significant role in managing their career, the effects of how you think and the way you behave aren't just limited to your own growth and success. It has a tremendous impact on others. When you're confident about yourself, believe in your potential, and are willing to do whatever it takes to move forward with the desire to find solutions, you become unstoppable. Your positive attitude creates a momentum that's hard to break. Your energy is infectious. Everyone around you feels the positive vibes. They're encouraged to think this way too. In this case, your domino effect cascades positivity and passion.

What happens though when you think and behave just the opposite? When you constantly doubt yourself and believe you're not good enough, your focus shifts from finding solutions to saving yourself. From learning to proving yourself. From moving forward to avoiding mistakes. Growth isn't even a discussion when it's all about survival. Being hyper-vigilant and constantly trying to avoid the bad leads to poor choices, terrible decisions, and exhaustion. Others around you get caught up in this way of thinking too. In this case, your domino effect cascades negativity and frustration.

While confidence in yourself creates the thrust that uplifts people, lack of it pulls them down. When a leader at the helm suffers from imposter syndrome, the entire organization can feel its effects. If you aren't careful, your fears of feeling like an imposter can lead to dysfunctional behaviors that can shatter team dynamics and impact company performance.

This is how imposter thinking in a leader can impact its employees and destroy the company's culture:

THINKING/ BEHAVIOR	IMPACT	EFFECT
Constantly worried about what others will think	Poor decision-making	Makes them less likely to go with an unpopular opinion even if it's the right thing to do as they fear standing apart
Give too much weight to the worst-case scenario	Decreases their appetite to take risks	Avoid new opportunities and challenges because they are more focused on survival than growth
Set extremely high standards for others	Become intolerant to imperfection	Fail to achieve desired outcomes as it's impossible to achieve their levels of unrealistic perfection
Avoid appearing foolish	Limits their ability to speak up or have honest conversations	Others often don't know what they are thinking which causes mis-alignment and unresolved differences of opinion
Stay away from vulnerability	Become ignorant to blind spots	Not knowing enough and believing that they need to know everything builds resistance to ask for help, slows them down and can even cause analysis paralysis
Desire to	Micromanaging	Willing to do whatever it

control everything	and fault-finding	takes to avoid mistakes with the thinking that any mistake will reflect on their competence, which leads to low productivity, heightened stress, and reduced creativity in people
Regularly work late	Promote overwork	Employees constantly feel under pressure to work harder and longer which impacts their mental health and well-being
Punish mistakes	Risk aversion	Employees try to play safe, stay under the radar, and hide their mistakes instead of learning from them which creates a culture of fear as opposed to a culture of innovation

Roger Jones, chief executive of consulting firm Vantage Hill Partners, conducted a survey of 116 CEOs and other executives, of which 73 percent were male and 27 percent were female. In *Harvard Business Review*, he wrote about their most deep-seated fears and how those fears affected their business. His findings were revealing. According to the survey, the biggest fear of these CEOs and executives was "being found to be incompetent." He stated that feeling like an imposter not only diminished their confidence but also undermined their relationships with other executives. Deep and uncontrolled private fears spurred defensive behaviors that undermined how they and their colleagues set and executed company strategy.[3]

When you're in a position of leadership or when you're responsible for others, it may all seem a bit scary. Everything you do is in the spotlight which makes you highly visible and every mistake even harder to hide. It's also lonely at the top. Without the social support needed to deal with the pressures of the job, you may feel isolated. You probably had the support and the mentoring from senior executives all along, but now you are one of them and expected to stand on your own. Combine this with high expectations and high levels of responsibility and it won't be surprising to know that so many leaders feel like an imposter in their roles.

But remember this. Your imposter feelings show up because you're trying to do something worthwhile. You can't possibly know everything. You can't be decisive and yet never make mistakes. Even with the best of intentions, you can make decisions that can hurt your organization and its people. When the job shows up with new expectations and unexpected surprises, you can't hold back and be scared. Without experiencing the ups and downs, you can never get over your fears and build the confidence and skills required to succeed in life.

In his famous TEDx talk, *I am Enough*, Fred Johnson says "Why would people invest themselves in us and our causes and those things that are meaningful to us? It's because at some point in time you believed in them. And when people know that they're believed in, they respond to those who are believers. Not only did you believe in them, but they began to believe in you. And where did all that start? It started from your ability to believe in yourself...Truly great leadership that has the ability to move the hearts and minds of people, to do beyond what they thought they were capable of takes someone to believe in them deeply and that is the reason why leadership always starts from within. It's an inside out job and you cannot lead other people until you lead yourself...You cannot lead people and push them away at the same time. Great leaders are willing to do the deep dives and look at themselves and say what are the behaviors in my life that I need to change and do I have the courage to take that deep look."[4]

Are you willing to practice the courage to do that deep dive? Are you ready to believe in yourself?

In the upcoming chapters, you'll find the 7-step process that will bridge the gap between where you're now to where you want to be. You'll find strategies that will make you thrive, and not simply survive. Managing your imposter feelings shouldn't only be about wanting better things for yourself, it should also be about feeling better about yourself. And that requires a profound shift in the way you think, behave and act.

Morpheus tells Neo in the movie *Matrix* that's so apt now "I can only show you the door. You're the one that has to walk through it." You can't deal with your feelings of self-doubt unless you're willing to walk through the door. Don't be surprised if what you see on the other side isn't as expected. You may have to cross many wrong doors before you get to the right ones. But trust you'll reach there. Be prepared to stick around. These strategies are only as effective as your willingness to practice.

This quote from Oprah Winfrey captures the idea well "You can either waltz boldly onto the stage of life and live the way you know your spirit is nudging you to, or you can sit quietly by the wall, receding into the shadows of fear and self-doubt." The choice is yours.

Chapter Summary

- If you're a leader or someone in a position to influence and impact others, your feelings of not being worthy and undeserving are not only harmful to you, they have a profound negative effect on others.
- Knowing that others look up to them, and have high expectations of them along with the other demands of the job makes many leaders prone to imposterism. They are constantly surrounded by feelings of self-doubt "What if I don't say the right thing, make the wrong choice, or act imperfectly?"
- While positivity and confidence in a leader inspire others to take risks, learn from their mistakes and put their best foot forward, negativity and lack of confidence from imposter feelings tell them to play safe, avoid mistakes and keep their heads down.
- Imposter syndrome in a leader causes a domino effect in an entire organization. Their limiting beliefs not only pull them down, their behavior inadvertently knocks down everyone else too.
- Your job as a leader isn't to know everything, make the perfect decision, or always say the right thing. That's unrealistic and impossible. Your job is to build a culture where employees are encouraged to bring their authentic selves to work, motivated to do their best work, and not let their doubts get in the way of their success.
- Don't sit around and expect great things to happen. Believe in yourself and do the work that's necessary to regain your confidence.

Part 3

Overcoming Imposter Syndrome

CHAPTER 9

Step 1: Acknowledge the Elephant in the Room

WHAT DO YOU DO when someone close to you hurts you, disappoints you, or makes you mad? Do you avoid them or confront them? Years of learning to ignore and avoid bad things can make confrontation appear risky and scary. But ignoring this bad experience does not make things better or how you feel about them. The more you put off dealing with or even acknowledging that something is wrong, the worse it becomes. Psychologists call it emotional avoidance. Avoiding negative emotions makes you feel better. Avoidance provides a momentary relief from negative emotions which is effective in the short term, but it makes whatever you were avoiding bigger in the long term.

Negative emotions may show up when you're:

- Passed up for a promotion
- Subjected to discrimination
- Being yelled at by your boss
- Receive criticism
- Made to work long hours
- Ignored or avoided by your friends
- Fail to meet others' expectations

How do you deal with negative emotions—try to hide them and make them go away or acknowledge the moment they happen? When you do not acknowledge negative emotions, your body's built-in defense mechanism treats them as a threat. Once activated, your body releases stress hormones like cortisol and adrenaline which causes you to act in one of the following ways:

You fight the threat: Try to fight your emotions which makes them more intense.

You flight from the situation: Try hard to dismiss the emotion, often wasting energy that's best spent on some constructive action.

This fight-or-flight response is vital to our survival in other circumstances when there's real danger as it enables us to respond to life-threatening situations quickly—to escape a burning building or when a speeding car on a highway heads into our lane. However, since your brain can't differentiate between real and perceived threats, it can set off the alarm bells even when it's just an emotional attack and in the process restrict access to the prefrontal cortex, which is the thinking part of your brain inhibiting purposeful action exactly when you need it the most.

Avoidance is like a prison. Once it becomes a way of life, you may start ignoring all the challenges and opportunities that may stir up negative emotions. That prevents you from experiencing critical life lessons. You fail to build the skills necessary to deal with discomfort. Every repeated cycle of negative emotions leading to avoidance makes it powerful and weakens your ability to deal with difficult situations. Noam Shpancer, professor of psychology at Otterbein University and a clinical psychologist specializing in the treatment of anxiety disorders says "Attempts at avoiding negative emotions are usually futile. Telling yourself that a certain emotion is intolerable or dangerous traps you in constant vigilance regarding the very thing you're trying to avoid. You become hyper-vigilant about any possibility of this feeling arising. The fear of the impending negative experience becomes a negative experience in itself."[1]

This applies to how you deal with your imposter feelings as well. Instead of confronting your feelings, you may believe that the best way to deal with them is to put them out of your mind. But ignoring or avoiding makes these feelings much harder to overcome, while acknowledging them can result in real personal growth. Instead of stifling or pushing them away, what if you learn to accept your emotions? Accepting does not make them true. It just allows your emotions to be what they are without judging them or trying to change them. Seeing the emotion for what it is without attempting to get rid of it shifts you from emotional avoidance towards emotional acceptance.

EMOTIONAL AVOIDANCE

Avoiding emotions creates a lot of noise

EMOTIONAL ACCEPTANCE

Accepting emotions makes you calm

Noam Shpancer calls emotional acceptance a far better strategy than avoidance because accepting, acknowledging, and absorbing them makes you spend less energy in pushing the emotion away and instead pursue the behaviors that are aligned with your goals and values. He says "Emotions, when viewed as part of a spectrum of available sources of information, are a bit like the weather report. They are important to know, consider, and understand, but they are not necessarily the overriding factor in your life plans. When the weather is bad (not to your liking), it doesn't mean you have to deny it, focus all your attention on it, or cancel your plans because of it. What you need to do is accept the weather and adjust your plans accordingly."

Tara Brach, psychologist and author tells a story about Buddha and demon Mara[2] in her book *Radical Acceptance* which goes like this: Buddha's loyal attendant Ananda was always on the lookout for any harm that might come to his teacher. One day, he noticed that Mara, the evil one, had returned with plans to wreak havoc. When Ananda warned Buddha of Mara's presence, instead of ignoring Mara or driving him away, Buddha calmly acknowledged his presence and said "I see you, Mara." He invited Mara for tea, offered him a cushion so that he could sit comfortably, and filled two earthen cups with tea. Mara stayed for a while and then went away, but throughout Buddha remained free and undisturbed.

This story beautifully captures how you should respond to feelings of inadequacy and not being good enough. Tara suggests to embrace your hurts and fears which apply to your imposter feelings as well "Just as a relationship with a good friend is marked by understanding and compassion, we can learn to bring these same qualities to our own inner life. When Mara visits us, in the form of troubling emotions or fearsome stories, we can say, "I see you, Mara," and clearly recognize the reality of craving and fear that lives in each human heart. By accepting these experiences with the warmth of compassion, we offer Mara tea rather than fearfully driving him away. Seeing what is true, we hold what is seen with kindness."

It's about not resisting your emotions. It's about feeling them completely and yet not turning over your choices to them. This is the first and most essential step to manage your imposter feelings instead of letting the voice in your head own you. Next time, when you face feelings of self-doubt, when you feel incompetent, or when you try to give up with feelings of not being good enough, let those feelings in. Acknowledge how you are feeling without rushing to change your emotional state. Instead of backing away from negative emotions, accept and acknowledge your irrational fears. Invite them, give them space to settle in, and then say it out loud "Welcome back my old friend. I see you're here. Now come in."

Brené Brown, author of *Rising Strong* says "The opposite of recognizing that we're feeling something is denying our emotions. The opposite of being curious is disengaging. When we deny our stories and disengage from tough emotions, they don't go away; instead, they own us, they define us. Our job is not to deny the story, but to defy the ending—to rise strong, recognize our story, and rumble with the truth until we get to a place where we think, Yes. This is what happened. This is my truth. And I will choose how this story ends."[3]

Acknowledging your imposter feelings in this way has multiple advantages:

- It sends a strong, calming signal to your autonomic nervous system.
- Instead of internalizing the emotions, recognizing them gets you prepared to move on.
- Negative emotions from feeling like an imposter stop hounding you when you give them the attention.
- You recognize that your feelings might be unhelpful but they are surprisingly normal.
- By acknowledging these thoughts, you begin to unravel the faulty beliefs that are holding you back.

Now that you've acknowledged the elephant in the room, it's time to give it a voice.

BREAK THE SILENCE

Acknowledging your imposter feelings has two parts. One is an internal acknowledgment where you accept your emotions without judgment; where you let them in just like Buddha invited Mara to tea. Another form of acknowledgment is outside you where you share how you're feeling with others. Externalizing the noise in your head can create a distance or a separation that reduces the intensity of the thought. Talking to someone trusted, someone who knows you and supports you can help you realize that your imposter feelings are a normal part of life's experience. When you share your imposter feelings, others are bound to share their experience too. It can be reassuring to know that you're not the only one to feel this way and others are sharing the burden with you. Knowing that this is not just unique to you will make it feel less intimidating and make you more open to talking about it and seeking others' opinions.

Once you get your imposter feelings out of your head into the open, it stops rumination—a pattern of circling thoughts which consumes you. Breaking the silence weakens its power to peck at your confidence. It can be freeing to get intrusive thoughts out by telling them to your sounding board.

Here are some of the ways to give voice to your imposter feelings:

BREAK THE SILENCE
Talk candidly about your struggles with imposter syndrome. **Start with a safe environment**: a mentor or a trusted advisor. People from similar professions or similar working conditions are usually better equipped to understand your feelings. Richard Gardner, PhD, and an assistant professor of management, entrepreneurship, and technology at the University of Nevada says that airing

impostor struggles with peers can promote comparison and increase the imposter phenomenon, but sharing your imposter feelings with trusted individuals outside your professional circle can provide a more helpful picture of your accomplishments and value.[4]
For people with underrepresented identities, Andrea Salazar-Nuñez, PhD, and a clinical psychologist at the University of Washington Counseling Center suggests that it can be helpful to **connect in empowering spaces and communities**, which can provide support and, more important, validation and empathy for navigating imposter phenomenon.[5]
Invest in **creating a network of mutual support**. Your network can offer guidance and support, validate your strengths and encourage you to grow.

When you're ready to face your fears, share your insecurities and express your vulnerability. Other people will relate to you and they will be much more forthcoming about the mistakes they've made and the imposter struggles they've faced in their own careers. Some might even share helpful advice on how to deal with negative emotions. Knowing that others have been in your position makes your feelings less scary and reassures you that what you're feeling is normal.

That's what Alvin Tan, Minister of State for Culture, Community, and Youth for the Republic of Singapore did. Alvin felt like an imposter many times in his career. From starting out as an associate in an investment bank in Hong Kong to corporate leadership in a tech company to being asked to serve his country as

Minister of State, he felt like an imposter all along. Every time he took on a new role, those feelings would return. It was overwhelming. To get over his imposter feelings, he stopped concealing how he felt and instead talked about it. He learned that he was not the only one, some of his peers felt the same way "I had fellow students who felt that they were admitted because of an admissions error, junior bankers who worried they weren't good enough to make it in the world of finance, and even fellow corporate leaders who later revealed their struggles with self-doubt."[6]

Alvin also asked for help. He sought mentors to learn from who would coach him. Many agreed to take him under their wing and mentor him. He learned how to speak up in class and at work, drive projects, and lead with and without formal authority. Over time, he got better, learned more, got more confident in his role, and started mentoring others. Alvin Tan's story demonstrates the power of facing your emotions by letting them in and sharing them with others instead of suffering in silence.

Let's do this exercise to help you put this step into practice. The exercise will guide you to shift from emotional avoidance towards emotional acceptance.

Exercise: Inviting Mara to Tea

This exercise is taken from the book *Radical Acceptance* by Tara Brach.[7]

Sitting quietly, close your eyes and take a few full breaths. Bring to mind a current situation that elicits a reaction of anger, fear or grief. It may be a rift with your partner, the loss of a loved one, a power struggle with your child, a chronic illness, a hurtful behavior that you now regret. The more fully you get in touch with the charged essence of the story, the more readily you can access the feelings in your heart and throughout your body. What is it about this situation that provokes the strongest feelings? You might see a particular scene in your mind, hear words that were spoken, recognize a belief you hold about how this situation reflects on you or what it means for your future. Be especially aware of the feelings in your stomach, chest and throat.

In order to see firsthand what happens when you resist experience, begin by experimenting with saying no. As you connect with the pain you feel in the situation you have chosen, mentally direct a stream of no at the feelings. No to the unpleasantness of fear, anger, shame or grief. Let the word carry the energy of no—rejecting, pushing away what you are experiencing. As you say no, notice what this resistance feels like in your body.

1. Do you feel tightness, pressure?
2. What happens to the painful feelings as you say no?
3. What happens to your heart?

Imagine what your life would be like if, for the next hours, weeks and months, you continued to move through the world with the thoughts and feelings of no.

Take a few deep breaths and let go by relaxing through the body, opening your eyes or shifting your posture a bit. Now take a few moments to call to mind again the painful situation you'd previously chosen, remembering the images, words, beliefs and feelings connected with it. This time let yourself be the Buddha under the bodhi tree, the Buddha inviting Mara to tea. Direct a stream of the word yes at your experience. Agree to the experience with yes. Let the feelings float, held in the environment of yes. Even if there are waves of no—fear or anger that arise with the painful situation or even from doing this exercise—that's okay. Let these natural reactions be received in the larger field of yes. Yes to the pain. Yes to the parts of us that want the pain to go away. Yes to whatever thoughts or feelings arise. Notice your experience as you say yes.

1. Is there softening, opening and movement in your body?
2. Is there more space and openness in your mind?
3. What happens to the unpleasantness as you say yes? Does it get more intense? Does it become more diffuse?
4. What happens to your heart as you say yes?

What would your experience be in the hours, weeks and months to come, if you could bring the spirit of yes to the inevitable challenges and sorrows of life?

Continue to sit now, releasing thoughts and resting in an alert, relaxed awareness. Let your intention be to say a gentle YES to whatever sensations, emotions, sounds or images may arise in your awareness.

After applying this exercise to different emotional experiences in your life, repeat it for the emotions you feel when you experience feelings of self-doubt. Once you're comfortable acknowledging your imposter feelings to yourself, look for a safe environment and practice sharing these feelings with others. Ask them if they've ever felt this way, or if they know someone who has. Discuss the common triggers and identify areas where you feel stuck.

Your feelings of being an imposter won't go away yet, but acknowledging and accepting them will create the space necessary to move forward with the next steps.

You can download a printable version of "Inviting Mara to Tea" at:
techtello.com/rethink-imposter-syndrome/worksheets/

If you've trouble accepting your emotions at first, remember this from Mary Anne Radmacher, a writer and an artist who said "Courage doesn't always roar. Sometimes courage is the little voice at the end of the day that says I'll try again tomorrow." You may not be able to fully accept your emotions today, maybe not even tomorrow. But if you keep trying and don't give up, you'll learn to embrace your emotions. Every step will create the mindset shift required to realize your strengths, own your accomplishments and believe in your power to create your own path to success as opposed to letting your thoughts govern where you end up.

What do you think about mistakes and failures? Do you give up when the going gets tough or do you persist? Do you try to seek feedback or avoid criticism? How you view mistakes and failures greatly determines how you feel about them when they do happen and whether you feel helpless and hopeless or determined to take action. Combine this with how you feel about yourself—inept, incapable, not good enough—and your feelings of inadequacy can easily get in the way of pursuing a difficult challenge. But you can turn this around. In the next chapter, you'll learn to not only deal with setbacks when they do happen but also actively seek difficult challenges and opportunities with the mindset to learn from them.

Chapter Summary

- When you reject, deny or ignore your imposter feelings, those feelings do not go away. Negative rumination and stress that comes from dismissing your emotions only makes them worse.

- Negative emotions from feeling like a fake alerts your body. Your brain, not knowing what to do, thinks it's about survival. It tightens you up and chokes you down. Fight-or-flight mechanisms fire up. It creates a physiological response to either fight the emotion or run away from it.
- Avoiding your imposter feelings even if they're unhelpful does not make them better. Emotional avoidance makes them worse while emotional acceptance, learning to be more aware and accepting of your emotions gives them the space needed to see them for what they're without judging them or trying to change them.
- Acknowledging your emotions doesn't make them true. Apart from helping you calm down, they help you see that these emotions are a part of human experience. Knowing that you have a choice to own your experience without letting it own you makes you better prepared to move on.
- Knowing that you're not alone in feelings of fraudulence is not enough. You actually need to talk about it to get past it and feel less lonely. Once you've acknowledged your imposter feelings to yourself, share them with a mentor or a trusted advisor. Ask them about their imposter experience. What struggles did they face? What mistakes did they make? What strategies worked for them?
- A healthy dialogue with people you trust can offer support and often serve as a reminder that your imposter feelings are a creation of your mind and not really facts.

CHAPTER 10

Step 2: Stop Treating Mistakes As Personal Failings

NO ONE'S PERFECT. Everyone faces failures and makes mistakes from time to time. However, for people with imposter syndrome, mistakes and failures are not a normal part of life but rather something to avoid. With the mindset that every mistake reflects on your competence and every failure exposes your inadequacies to others, it's hard to consider them as a medium for growth. Personalizing your experience makes them about you as opposed to your work. Thinking it's you who's the source of the problem makes it much harder for you to move on when these mistakes do happen.

Think for a moment about which of these apply to you.

- When someone criticizes your work, you consider it as proof that you're a fraud.
- You fixate on the past and have a hard time accepting and letting go of even small mistakes.
- When things go wrong or don't work out as expected, you constantly criticize yourself.

- You experience a fear of failure so intense that it often hinders your ability to make the right decision.
- You have a tendency to obsess about what you said and how you said it.
- When voicing your opinion, you worry that less than a perfect answer will expose your ineptness.

Epictetus, a Greek Stoic philosopher once said "It's not what happens to you, but how you react to it that matters."[1] In other words, you will fail and make mistakes many times. You will also face criticism. What matters is how you see them, how you react to them, and whether you choose to stay calm as opposed to giving in to your feelings of fear and powerlessness which hurts your self-confidence.

Consider these examples.

Let's say your boss asks you to put together the prototype of a new product in a week's time. Despite your best effort, you fail to meet the requirements. Even though it was a prototype that failed, you may start considering yourself a failure. Assuming ownership of the failure by identifying what went wrong makes you better prepared to handle such opportunities next time. However, thinking that it didn't work out because you're incompetent leaves no room for improvement. No amount of hard work can fix the problem when you think it's a capability issue.

In another instance, your boss calls you one morning to share feedback on your last deliverable. When she points out areas where your work is not good enough, you personalize that criticism. Thinking this reflects on who you are as a person makes you interpret "Your work is not good enough" to mean "You're not good enough." Recognizing areas where your work needs improvement gives you an opportunity to advance your performance while internalizing the criticism and treating it as a confirmation of your deficiencies gives rise to feelings of shame and embarrassment.

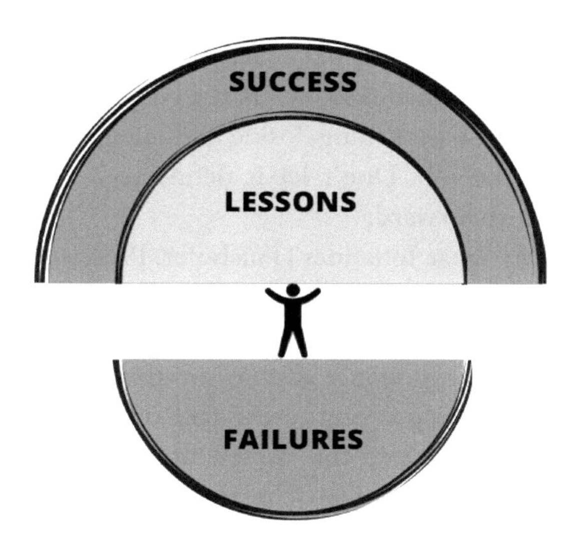

VIEW FAILURES AS STEPPING STONES TO SUCCESS

The real problem isn't failing—it's when these failures convince you to stop trying. Treating mistakes as personal failings unconsciously sabotages your chances of success. When criticism evokes strong negative emotions, you start associating anything risky or challenging with those emotions. You want to stay away from these feelings at all costs. The negative emotions of anger, disappointment, and inadequacy that often accompany mistakes and failures make you want to avoid them. You give up on opportunities you are well-suited to perform. You think it's better to play safe and stay under the radar than risk exposure.

When some part of your effort fails, it's rarely the end of the world. Being occasionally wrong, failing, and not knowing everything does not make you fake or undeserving. It only makes you human. Even the most accomplished people have room for improvement. Making mistakes is inevitable. If you learn from those mistakes, it's okay to fail every now and then. As Jessica Bennett points out in a *New York Times* article "Failure doesn't make you a fraud. Even the best athletes screw up, the best lawyers lose cases, the best actors star in busts. Failing, losing and being wrong on occasion are all part of the job. Don't let it define you. Learn from your mistakes and move forward."[2]

This is exactly what Johannes Haushofer, Professor of Economics at the Department of Economics, Stockholm University did. He published his "CV of failures"[3] online in an attempt to make others realize that we all experience failure on the way to success and encourage them to keep trying in the face of disappointment. The document stretches back to the late-1990s, and details every single academic rejection letter, failed scholarship application, unaccepted degree program, and turned-down job position that he's had to deal with to get to where he is now. Haushofer wrote that he created the document to give some perspective "Most of what I try fails, but these failures are often invisible, while the successes are visible. I have noticed that this sometimes gives others the impression that most things work out for me. As a result, they are more likely to attribute their own failures to themselves, rather than the fact that the world is stochastic, applications are crapshoots, and selection committees and referees have bad days. This CV of Failures is an attempt to balance the record and provide some perspective."

How can knowing others' failures help us? In one experiment conducted by a team of researchers from Columbia University, 402 students were divided into three groups.[4] The first group read a typical, 800-word science textbook description about the great accomplishments of Albert Einstein, Marie Curie, and Michael Faraday, an English scientist who made important contributions in the fields of electromagnetism and electrochemistry. Instead of learning about their achievements, a second group read about the scientists' personal struggles, such as Marie Curie having to deal with being barred from university for being a woman and Albert Einstein fleeing from Nazi Germany for being a Jew. The third group read about the scientists' intellectual struggles, such as Curie's many failed experiments, and Einstein's multiple school changes and problems convincing his peers that gravity could actually bend light, and how they overcame them.

At the end of the six weeks, the experiment concluded with three major findings:

- Students who learned of the scientists' struggles, intellectual failures and experiments gone wrong (second and third groups) ended up outperforming the group that learned only of their achievements.
- Lowest performing students in the 'struggle story' groups (second and third groups) ended up making the greatest gains in their grades.
- Students who learned only about the scientists' achievements (first group) performed worse.

This research experiment shows that recognizing other people's failures can break down the shame and humiliation often associated with mistakes and failures and inspire you to work harder. When presented with a new opportunity, if the voice in your head says "Don't do it...you will fail," remind yourself of everyone who succeeded despite failing initially. Taking on challenging work and new opportunities can be a game-changer to help you learn, grow and advance in your career.

STOP BEING GOOD, START GETTING BETTER

Knowing everyone fails is motivating, but it's sometimes not enough. There's another factor that can get in the way. Heidi Grant, a social psychologist at EY and Columbia's Motivation Science Center says that the types of goals you set for yourself play a crucial role in determining how you deal with difficulty when it happens—whether you'll be persistent and determined or feel overwhelmed and helpless.[5] She describes two types of goals "being good" and "getting better" and says they determine not only your motivation level but also how long you'll persist when the going gets tough. *Being good* goals are also called performance goals while *getting better* goals are referred to as setting learning goals.

Here are the main differences between the two types of goals:[6]

PERFORMANCE GOALS (BEING GOOD)	LEARNING GOALS (GETTING BETTER)
Focus on self-validation: performing well to prove that you're good at what you do. Show that you're smart, talented, and capable or to outperform other people.	Focus on self-improvement: progress, growth, and gaining mastery. Becoming the best, most capable person you can be, rather than proving that you already are.
Energy is directed at achieving a particular outcome. Meeting the outcome is the primary criteria to determine whether you're successful or not.	Energy is directed at acquiring knowledge or skill and the progress you're making. How much you're improving. What you're learning. It's all about the journey, less about any one

	performance and more about performance over time.
Not achieving the desired outcome shakes your confidence. You may feel embarrassed and ashamed or anxious and depressed.	You are less likely to get depressed because you don't see setbacks and failures as reflecting on your own self-worth. You are also less likely to stay depressed because feeling bad makes you want to work harder and keep striving.
Blame difficulties and poor performance on lack of ability which makes you give up without trying hard enough.	Increase your effort, use better strategies, and seek the right kind of help when you need it which makes you persist in the face of difficulties.
Avoid asking for help because it seems like an admission of failure and makes you look incompetent.	Consider asking for help as an excellent way to get better.
Hold back from risks or putting yourself into challenging situations with fear of failure. You only pick opportunities you're confident you can meet.	Insert yourself in difficult situations and pick ever-increasing challenges to build and practice new skills.

Carol Dweck, a Professor of Psychology at Stanford University who discovered a simple but groundbreaking idea about the power of mindsets says that with a performance mindset, which people suffering from imposter syndrome often have "you tend to see your feelings of inadequacy or the mistakes you make as evidence of your underlying limitations. This mindset only fuels the concerns you have about being unfit for your job. But there's something you can work to cultivate instead: a learning mindset. From this perspective, your limitations are experienced quite differently. Your mistakes are seen as an inevitable part of the learning process rather than as more evidence of your underlying failings."[7]

With performance goals, you're more likely to set yourself with unrealistic and unsustainable expectations of performance and think you're a failure when you do not reach them.

I am a failure if I did not get into a specific school.

I am a failure if my scholarship essay is rejected.
I am a failure if my book is not a bestseller.
I am a failure if I get rejected by my dream company.

Holding yourself to that standard can be counterproductive. You not only fail to achieve the unrealistic goal, you also declare yourself a failure and stop trying. Unable to test your own skills and abilities realistically makes you feel ashamed and frustrated. This further reinforces your imposter feelings which have been telling you that "you're not good enough" all along.

With learning goals, you're less focused on achieving a certain outcome and more on enhancing your skills and abilities. It's about resetting the expectations to align with the progress you're making—how much are you improving each day? What strategies are working? What solutions do you need to implement to get over the unexpected obstacles and challenges? When learning is the goal, you pay more attention to the process, find work more interesting and experience a sense of joy which leads to even higher levels of motivation.

Now for the interesting question: Should you never set performance goals? Not really. Performance goals are good when you find something relatively easy to do. Trying to prove that you're good at what you do can be very motivating and lead to excellent performance. However, when doing something unfamiliar or complex like working on a new task or a challenge, you're more likely to face setbacks. In those situations, persistence is what's needed to succeed. It's also when your imposter feelings are likely to show up. In those cases, you're better off with learning goals. In general, whenever possible, set yourself learning goals instead of performance goals.

- Instead of the goal to sell hundred units a week, learn how to become a better salesperson.
- Instead of the goal to acquire thousand new customers, learn how to build the best product.
- Instead of the goal to secure a million dollars funding, learn how to hone and produce your best pitch.
- Instead of the goal to become a millionaire by selling a business, learn how to create the most successful business.
- Instead of the goal to win an award for the best employee of the month, learn how to produce your best work.

This in no way means that you shouldn't care about the outcomes. Rather, learning goals lead to far superior performance. It's just a shift in perspective in which instead of judging yourself solely on the outcomes, you care more about the learning. By setting learning goals as opposed to performance goals, you adopt the mindset of a lifelong learner. When you feel self-doubt or that you're not good enough, learning goals will snap you out from feeling discouraged and inspire you to push ahead knowing that you can get past the challenges and obstacles only if you keep trying. Even if success seems far-fetched, you're more likely to persist knowing fully well that improvement is still possible and that you can still learn.

Let's do this exercise to change the way you think about mistakes and failures.

Exercise: Change Your Relationship With Failure

This is a 3-part exercise. In part 1, you'll look at your current goals and identify which goals you pursue more—performance or learning goals. In part 2, you'll do goals reframing by turning your performance goals into learning goals. Finally, in part 3, you will learn to see the value of failures through your own experience.

Part 1: Which goals do you pursue more?

Take a moment to read each of the statements below and select the choice that best describes your response using a 5-point scale (1 - Not at all true, 2 - rarely, 3 - sometimes, 4 - often, and 5 - very true). Try to be completely honest. Remember, there are no right or wrong answers. What matters is that you stay true to yourself when you attempt this exercise.

No.	STATEMENT	1	2	3	4	5
1	I like to be surrounded by people who can give me feedback and help me learn.					
2	I constantly strive to outperform others.					
3	I seek opportunities that challenge me to build new skills.					
4	I am more focused on doing work that demonstrates my ability and proves my smartness.					
5	I persist when I face setbacks and look for new ways to solve the problem and move forward.					
6	I give up as soon as it gets tough or					

	when it seems like I am going to fail.					
7	I care less about others' opinions of me and more about what I am learning and whether I am improving.					
8	I consider others' validation as a measure of my self-worth.					
9	I consider mistakes and failures as a sign to increase effort, try a new strategy, or ask for help.					
10	I consider mistakes and failures as a sign of my incompetence.					

To calculate your learning goals score: Add up your scores from rows 1, 3, 5, 7, and 9 above. Divide this by 5.

To calculate your performance goals score: Add up your scores from rows 2, 4, 6, 8, and 10 above. Divide this by 5.

My performance goals score is _______________

My learning goals score is _______________

Which score is higher?

Part 2: Reframing goals

What all performance goals do you pursue? Think about them and turn them into learning goals. Use the space below to write your performance goal in the first column. Then think about a corresponding learning goal and write it in the second column. Keep a digital version of these "goals reframing" on your phone. Next time when you find yourself pursuing a performance goal, look up the corresponding learning goal and shift to that.

CURRENT PERFORMANCE GOAL	NEW LEARNING GOAL

Part 3: Experiencing failure

Think about a recent time when you failed at something. Now, think about a few positive things you learned from that experience. If you're someone who considered failures *bad* so far, it may take some time for you to think about the positive side of this experience. But, if you try hard, you can see that there's always something to learn even from the most difficult experiences in your life. Now, write it down.

Repeat this exercise every time your imposter syndrome makes you want to give up on an opportunity with the fear of failure by reframing "What will happen if I fail?" to "What can I learn?" By reframing your performance goals to learning goals and thinking about the positive side of every experience, you will stop considering mistakes and failures as a sign of your limitation and instead use them as an opportunity to build new skills and get better.

DESCRIBE YOUR FAILURE	POSITIVE THINGS YOU LEARNED FROM THIS EXPERIENCE

You can download a printable version of "Change Your Relationship With Failure" at:
techtello.com/rethink-imposter-syndrome/worksheets/

Every mistake is a learning lesson only if you give yourself the mental space to reflect on what happened or as sports psychologist Gerry Hussey puts it "See the world as one big learning opportunity, where you're going to fail, but you're going to get back up."[8] Once you stop considering mistakes and failures as a backward step, and start looking at them as a means to move ahead, you focus more on what you're learning than how you're performing. Your imposter feelings can't get in the way of pursuing a difficult challenge once you change the meaning of failure—failure is no longer a threat, something to avoid, or something that brings negative emotions. It's evidence of a need for change—
rewrite your assumptions, try out a new strategy, put in more effort, implement a different practice, or a better process.

Imposter syndrome often makes people diminish their accomplishments. Instead of recognizing the good stuff and giving it the attention it deserves, you might dwell on the small elements you're unhappy about or anything that doesn't meet your expectations. This tendency to direct your attention to negative experiences while not recognizing and celebrating the good things makes it harder for you to take up new challenges. Self-doubt is bound to show up when you don't have evidence of the skills you possess. When you can't recall your achievements from the past, a feeling of ineptness or that you're not good enough gets in the way of making meaningful progress. In the next chapter, we will build the evidence that you're indeed capable, smart, and successful. You have what it takes to go after difficult challenges, new opportunities, or anything that you deem impossible.

Chapter Summary

- When you're worried about being exposed as a fraud, you strive for flawless performance. There's no room for any mistake or any failure because making them puts you in front of others and proves that you're indeed incompetent.
- You think that you're not good enough. But receiving criticism just pushes you over the edge. Feedback about your work personally reflects on who you're as a person. If your performance is lacking, then others must consider you deficient and incapable of improvement.
- Thinking this way creates a psychological connection between mistakes, failures, criticism, and negative emotions. You want to avoid these emotions at all costs. So, instead of embracing new opportunities and difficult challenges, you put them off. Playing safe reduces your risk of failing and provides a safety net against these negative feelings.

- Failing at something does not signal incompetence. Mistakes do not speak of your limitations. Receiving criticism isn't a confirmation of your lack of abilities. They all point towards only one thing: you're human.
- Failures and mistakes don't make you a fraud. Even the most successful and highly accomplished people failed on their way to success. It was their perseverance and ability to learn from their failures that made them successful. Don't let them define you. Learn from them and move forward.
- To embrace failures as a learning lesson, shift from proving you're smart and capable to showing interest in improving. Focus on what you're learning, and how you're growing. When you stop chasing a particular outcome (performance goals) and focus on the process (learning goals), you stay resilient in the face of challenges. The joy that comes with improvement motivates you to do even better.

CHAPTER 11

Step 3: Look Beyond the Emotion to the Evidence

LUVVIE AJAYI JONES is an author, speaker, and podcaster known for her wit, warmth, and perpetual truth-telling. Despite being a NYT bestselling author, and a keynote speaker at multiple conferences who had spoken in front of thousands of people, when she was offered to do a TED talk, she turned it down twice. Her imposter syndrome kicked in.[1] She wasn't going to take the stage, bomb, and embarrass herself. Her inner critic told her "Who do you think you're to just be jumping in at the last minute?" She convinced herself that she wasn't ready for this yet and maybe in a year she'll be ready to take that stage. She drafted a three-paragraph email expressing her regret for not being able to speak at TED, but right before sending it, she decided to call a friend.

Luvvie's friend asked her a question that shifted how she thought about herself "No, no, no. You have the credentials. You have the experience. It might be three weeks before TED, but they're asking you to do this because they believe that you can do it. So, you actually don't have the reason to turn it down. If your reason to turn down TED is that you're afraid of bombing, do you usually bomb?"

That question made Luvvie realize that she had done this a thousand times before. She had the experience to do it. She had evidence from her past performances where she did pretty well. So, she got on the stage and killed it. That TED talk got 8 million views all over the world and has been transcribed into 18 different languages. It has been till date one of her most consumed things.

This experience from almost turning down the TED talk to becoming one of her most popular things taught Luvvie a very valuable lesson "Impostor Syndrome absolutely lies to us and has us thinking that we are not ready, we are not qualified, we are not good for whatever the opportunity or thing is."[2] From her own experience, she suggests that even if you don't believe in yourself, you can believe in somebody else's belief in you "If you're like, "I don't know if I can do this," but you have four people (for example) saying, "No, no, you got this," and then you borrow from some of their belief. You can use that to push you forward."

Adam Grant, an organizational psychologist, supports Luvvie's idea. He calls imposter syndrome a paradox:

"Impostor syndrome is a paradox:
Others believe in you.
You don't believe in yourself.
Yet you believe yourself instead of them.
If you doubt yourself, shouldn't you also doubt your judgment of yourself?
When multiple people believe in you, it might be time to believe them."[3]

When you're consumed by self-doubt and find it hard to realistically assess your skills, go to others you trust. They can share the evidence to help you see how your fears are just a creation of your mind and not a true measure of your worth. When your not-so-helpful imposter thoughts discourage you from moving forward and try to pull you down, trusting other people's instincts over your own instincts is a wise thing to do. There's another way to think about this. People who are lending you their trust by giving you the job, asking you to take on a difficult challenge or do the presentation, are probably smart and intelligent. What's more likely—your judgment about yourself or the fact that they see you as a capable person who's fit for the job? Do you really think that you can fool all these smart people into believing that you are competent?

- Why would they hire you for a job if you have no skills?
- Why would you be asked to coach others if you have nothing to teach?
- Why would you be asked to manage a major deal if you can't pull it off?
- Why would you be asked to lead others if you can't be trusted with their growth?
- Why would they keep giving you more and more responsibilities if you already suck at what you do?
- Why would they ask you to take on a challenging project if they don't trust you to do it well?
- Why would you be given an opportunity to present in front of hundreds of people if you're going to be terrible?

If you don't have what it takes, shouldn't other people who are more confident, more capable, more intelligent, and more smart be given all these opportunities? Why does everyone around you think you're better than you do? Everyone can't be nice. Everyone can't lie. Everyone can't exaggerate the truth. Your boss, coworkers, family, relatives, friends, and coaches must see something that you're unwilling to see in you.

TRACK YOUR WINS

What evidence do you have that makes you less qualified than anyone else to do the job, coach others, get that raise, or take on that big project? I know what you're going to say:

I've been lucky so far.
I just work harder than everyone else.
I probably got in the right place at the right time.
I know some pretty influential people who helped me get here.
It's my charming personality that makes me more likable.
They probably made a mistake this time.

Anything, but your skills. When you feel like an imposter, one of the hardest things to grasp is how much of a role you have in your own success. You may attribute it to luck, hard work, or other such factors, when in fact your own knowledge, skills, and abilities had a lot to do with it. The problem with not internalizing your accomplishments is this: your brain can't register the proof of all the times when you did well in the past. Instead of the huge upside you gained from each experience, your imposter feelings make you cling to the small downsides.

For example:

- You forget how you pulled off a major project while remembering the struggle meeting its deadline.
- You forget the negotiation skills that got you a big account while recollecting how you almost lost it.
- You forget all the positive feedback you received on a project while obsessing about the small amount of criticism.

Your negative experiences are insignificant in comparison to your gains. But that's what lingers in your mind. When hit with a new challenge, there's absolutely nothing to fall back on. Rather, holding onto the negative stories makes it much harder for you to believe that you're indeed capable to take on that challenge or do that thing.

To overcome imposter feelings, look beyond the emotions to the real evidence. Acknowledge your achievements. Take a realistic look at what capabilities and strengths you possess.

Starting now, try out some of these things:

- Track your wins.
- Highlight the positives.
- Don't downplay your achievements.
- Celebrate your accomplishments, big and small.
- Practice taking compliments, don't shrug them aside.
- Share your success with people you trust.

Celebrating your achievements and telling others about them isn't boasting. It isn't about discrediting your weaknesses either. It requires accurately judging your abilities and not using excuses to justify your wins. When your imposter feelings make you disregard your success, look up the excuse from the first column below and consciously shift to acknowledge your win using the second column.

INSTEAD OF THESE EXCUSES	ACKNOWLEDGE YOUR WINS
I've been lucky.	Luck might open the right doors for you, but you're still the one who has to step through them. Your luck can't make you successful if you fail to act. It's a small component in your success. You wouldn't have come this far without the ability to do well.

I just work harder than everyone else.	Don't take your hard work for granted. Look for what makes that hard work possible—determination to do well, perseverance to stay with the challenge, and the attitude to never stop learning. Not everyone has these skills.
I probably got in the right place at the right time.	Probably once or twice, but what about those other times? How did you navigate uncertainty? How did you make decisions? What action did you take? A lot of effort still goes into making something work and you're the reason behind it.
I know some pretty influential people who helped me get here.	Others might have helped you along the way, but they helped you only because they recognized your potential. Being successful doesn't mean doing it alone. Asking for help when you need it and using that to advance forward is a very important skill.
It's my charming personality that makes me more likable.	This is definitely something to celebrate. It isn't easy to get others to like you. Let's be clear though: others won't offer you the job or trust you with a big project only because they like it. You have other skills which make you well suited

	for the job. Being likable is a bonus.
They probably made a mistake this time.	Such mistakes aren't common. Others can judge when you're up to the task/job/course and when you're not. The likelihood of them making this mistake is very low. What's more probable is that you're indeed capable and they saw it in you.

Let's do this exercise to recognize your strengths. Knowing them will guide you to use them more often and also serve as a reminder that you're indeed capable when dealing with feelings of self-doubt.

Exercise: Strengths Reflection

This exercise requires daily reflection for the first few weeks to recognize your strengths. Daily reflection is often more accurate as it puts you in touch with current events. Follow the steps below and write down your responses to identify your strengths.

Step1: Record your wins

Record answers in columns 1 and 2 for a few weeks.

WEEK [X]	What are your big or small achievements today?	What comments, emails, or feedback did you receive that positively reinforces

		your accomplishments?
MONDAY		
TUESDAY		
WEDNESDAY		
THURSDAY		
FRIDAY		
SATURDAY		
SUNDAY		

Step 2: Identify your strengths

Do this once you have sufficient data from step 1 to recognize your strengths.

If you were to look at the list of all achievements and feedback from step 1 assuming they're for someone else, what would you think?	What feedback and qualities from column 1 do you see repeated often? List them. If you don't find sufficient number of qualities yet, keep looking. Repeat the exercise in step 1 till you have 10-15 qualities identified.	What top 5 strengths from column 2 personally appeal to you?

Step 3: Back them up

For every strength identified in step 2, write down three things to back it up—anything that demonstrates that particular strength to be true.

STRENGTH	BACK UP DATA

You can download a printable version of "Strengths Reflection" at:

techtello.com/rethink-imposter-syndrome/worksheets/

Keep a copy of the last step with your strengths and backup data readily available to you. Now, whenever you find yourself consumed with feelings of self-doubt, just look up your strengths data as evidence that you're indeed capable and have what it takes to achieve success. Remember this though: You need to define what you expect from yourself without subjecting yourself to impossible high standards to achieve or as Steven Pressfield, an author puts it in his book *The War of Art* "Our job in this lifetime is not to shape ourselves into some ideal we imagine we ought to be, but to find out who we already are and become it."[4]

The reason your imposter feelings win over your desire to do well is because you've been feeding your brain with limiting thoughts. When faced with feelings of self-doubt, if you behave and act a certain way, those behaviors become your brain's default go-to strategy. Your brain learns through repetition and starts associating your feelings of unworthiness with your response to avoid failures, berate yourself for making a mistake, and try to play safe. Beneath your consciousness, it makes these decisions for you. In the next chapter, you'll learn how to flip this around through a powerful strategy which will create new connections in your brain—connections that will empower you instead of holding you back.

Chapter Summary

- When you can't recall your achievements from the past or your strengths that made success possible, every new challenge looks like a mountain to climb. You've climbed it before but now feel like an amateur.

- Consumed by feelings of self-doubt makes it harder for you to recognize your strengths. In such moments, relying on others you trust makes more sense. They can show the evidence that you're indeed worthy to take up a new opportunity or a challenge. Trusting their instincts over your own instincts gives you just the right push to let go of the fears, get on and do the thing.
- When you use excuses (luck, hard work, or other factors) to justify your wins, you reject all the evidence (your skills and abilities) that made success possible.
- Recognizing your skills and abilities requires acknowledging your accomplishments. You need to register them in your mind so that they are available to you when you need them.
- Celebrating your accomplishments by tracking your wins is a surefire way to curb the effects of imposter feelings. Instead of downplaying your achievements, practice taking compliments. Instead of hiding your success, share them with the people you trust. Doing this often strengthens these circuits in your brain. They build the evidence needed to fight against your feelings of unworthiness and not being good enough.
- By tracking daily wins and any feedback you receive that positively reinforces your achievements, you can recognize your strengths. Maintain a list of strengths with the data to back it up. They will serve as a reminder of all the skills and abilities you possess. You can use them as proof that you're indeed capable.

CHAPTER 12

Step 4: Rewire Your Brain

ONE EVENING AN OLD Cherokee told his grandson about a battle that goes on inside people. He said, "My son, the battle is between two wolves inside us all. One is Evil. It is anger, envy, jealousy, sorrow, regret, greed, arrogance, self-pity, guilt, resentment, inferiority, lies, false pride, superiority, and ego. The other is Good. It is joy, peace, love, hope, serenity, humility, kindness, benevolence, empathy, generosity, truth, compassion, and faith." The grandson thought about it for a minute and then asked his grandfather, "Which wolf wins?" The old Cherokee simply replied, "The one you feed."[1] The evil wolf in your case is your imposter syndrome. The more you feed it, the more it overpowers you and dictates your actions.

Neuropsychologist Donald Hebb said "Neurons that fire together wire together" to describe how pathways in our brain are formed and reinforced through repetition. Every experience, thought, feeling, and physical sensation triggers thousands of neurons, which form a neural network. When you repeat an experience over and over, the brain learns to trigger the same neurons each time.[2] This is also how habits are formed. The more you practice a certain habit, the stronger the neural pathways get over time, making those habits easier to perform. What works well for habits also applies to how you choose to deal with feelings of unworthiness, self-doubt, and not being good enough.

When haunted by feelings of self-doubt, if you focus on negative attributes—things you have done wrong, mistakes you have made, skills and abilities you don't possess—and respond to those feelings by telling yourself that you're indeed a fraud, then that negativity becomes embedded in your brain. The more you adopt self-sabotage behaviors to deal with your imposter feelings, the stronger those connections get.

YOUR BRAIN ON AUTOPILOT

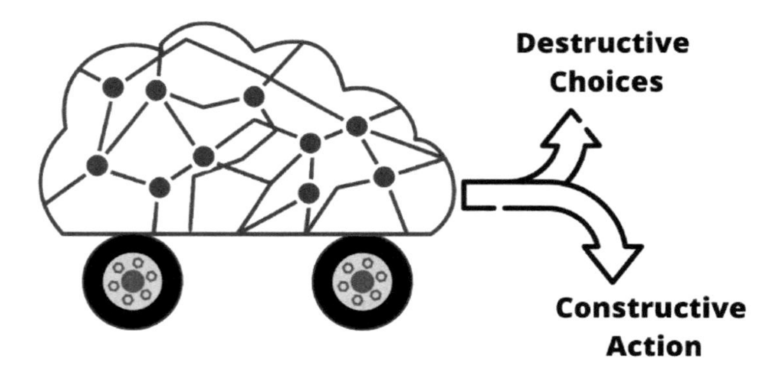

Your brain takes the path that you feed

Your brain runs on autopilot for a large part of your decisions. When struck by imposter feelings, feeding your brain with negativity makes it your default go-to strategy. Since the brain learns to make this decision beneath your consciousness, you may not even realize the harmful behaviors you adopt to deal with your feelings of inadequacy. They provide temporary relief but often limit your long-term potential.

For example, when repeated multiple times...

- If you tell yourself that speaking up in a meeting will expose you and choose to keep quiet, your brain learns to associate "keeping quiet" as a safe behavior while "speaking up" as a threat.
- When given an opportunity to lead, if you let it go with fear of failure, your brain learns to reject anything risky.
- If you disregard positive feedback or praise because you don't consider yourself worthy, your brain learns to diminish your other accomplishments too.
- When given a challenging task, if you keep delaying it with the fear that nothing you do can ever be good enough, your brain learns to put off difficult tasks automatically.

Since repetition is what builds new neural pathways in your brain, anything done multiple times becomes an unconscious truth for your brain. Jeffrey Schwartz, a psychiatrist, and researcher in the field of neuroplasticity and its application to obsessive-compulsive disorder writes in *You Are Not Your Brain* "What you do now and how you focus your attention influence your brain and how it is wired. Whenever you repeatedly avoid some kind of overtly painful sensation, your brain learns that these actions are a priority and generates thoughts, impulses, urges, and desires to make sure you keep doing them again and again. It does not care that the action ultimately is bad for you...This means that if you repeat the same act over and over—regardless of whether that action has a positive or negative impact on you—you make the brain circuits associated with that act stronger and more powerful."[3]

But you know what's the good news? Your brain has this amazing ability to change. You can overwrite old brain pathways with new preferred attitudes and behaviors. Instead of repeating self-defeating behaviors, you can reprogram the neural pathways in your brain to take constructive action. You can replace automatic shortcuts to negative thought patterns with positive strategies.

Once you unlearn old default behaviors and relearn new ways of being, when your imposter feelings strike, your brain recognizes those thoughts and the new pathways which allow you to step fully into your expertise. Whether it's asking for a raise, presenting to a large group, taking up a new job, or a challenge, your imposter feelings don't get in the way. Your new belief system reminds you of your credentials and tells you that you have the ability to do it. The new neural pathways in your brain help you recalibrate your perception of yourself and build the resilience needed to deal with your feelings of unworthiness. It enables you to recognize your inherent worth and acknowledge your accomplishments.

Michael Gervais is a sports psychologist who works with athletes in high stakes and consequential environments. He has worked with the Seattle Seahawks for eight years and with Felix Baumgartner, the Austrian who free dove from 130,000 feet as part of Red Bull's 2012 Stratos project. He says that what we say to ourselves matters. He suggests an increase in awareness of the narrative that is either constricting you or creating freedom "It's one of those two: constriction or freedom. And the more space we have, the more freedom we have to play, usually the better things go in all facets of life."[4]

To choose freedom over constriction, you need to reframe your thinking. You have to do the work to create new pathways in your brain. Simply saying positive affirmations like "I am amazing" or "I am capable" won't make your fears disappear. They are in direct conflict with your deeply held core beliefs that you're not enough and unworthy of success. Also, positive thinking works at the conscious part of the brain, while negative self-talk and limiting beliefs operate out of the subconscious mind. That's where you need to tap. You don't need positive thinking; you need to reframe your negative thoughts.

REFRAME YOUR THINKING

Leigh McBean, a former professional athlete turned lawyer, held a series of high-pressure management roles throughout his career. Once he was pulled out of an existing role and assigned to a major distribution center that ordered goods and sent them across the state in bulk. He was asked to map the warehouse layout, the path of the forklifts, how the pickers received their instructions, the stock placement on the shelves, the loading of the orders into containers, and then manage the logistics with the drivers, yet he had no relevant experience at the time. On his first day, he remembers going into the bathroom feeling quite ill and very much like an imposter who would be found out as someone who knew not much at all "It was outside my comfort zone, I felt like I was in the wrong place and that someone had made a mistake."[5]

Instead of letting his imposter feelings screw up this great opportunity in front of him, he decided to deal with the overwhelming discomfort he was experiencing "I acknowledged the feelings, firstly, and took a big breath...I thought about why I was there—it was partly because I had no experience in those areas that I was asked to do the role because they specifically wanted a fresh perspective from someone who could ask good questions and build rapport with people." What worked for Leigh? Reframing his thoughts from considering his inexperience as a flaw to a gift and from an obstacle to an opportunity helped subside his imposter feelings.

Yunita Ong was one of the youngest students among her cohort at Columbia University, Graduate School of Journalism. She was also one of the few who entered the program straight from undergrad without full-time working experience. She doubted herself heavily at the beginning. With journalists who were decades-long industry experts as her classmates, she questioned if she belonged and whether she could deliver on the program's requirements. She felt nervous to offer her opinions in class and whenever she did, she felt her classmates were more eloquent. But then Yunita learned a very powerful lesson: to not see imposter syndrome as something to suppress or ignore, but as a helpful ally. Over the academic year and during her career, whenever her imposter feelings surfaced, she used them as a signal to reframe those feelings of self-doubt "I started seeing it as my brain's way of telling myself I have an opportunity to transform beyond anything I can imagine at this current point. Now, I find it easier to replace my fear with excitement when embarking on a new journey. I also see it as my brain trying to help me. I pause to identify: What areas are there for me to learn and grow? What parts of my worry may not be valid? And I remember to identify the ways I can bring my strengths to the table as well."[6]

Leigh McBean and Yunita Ong rewired their brain by reframing their thoughts. Instead of considering their feelings of self-doubt as lack of their abilities, they used them as a signal to use their knowledge and skills to do well. By consciously tapping into their thoughts, they were able to reframe and change their subconscious-level thoughts as well which often run on autopilot.

You need to do the same. You need to train your brain to think differently. You need to build new neural pathways by adopting new ways of connecting with your thoughts and purposefully taking action. Once your brain learns these new ways of being, it won't let your imposter feelings take you away from your true goals.

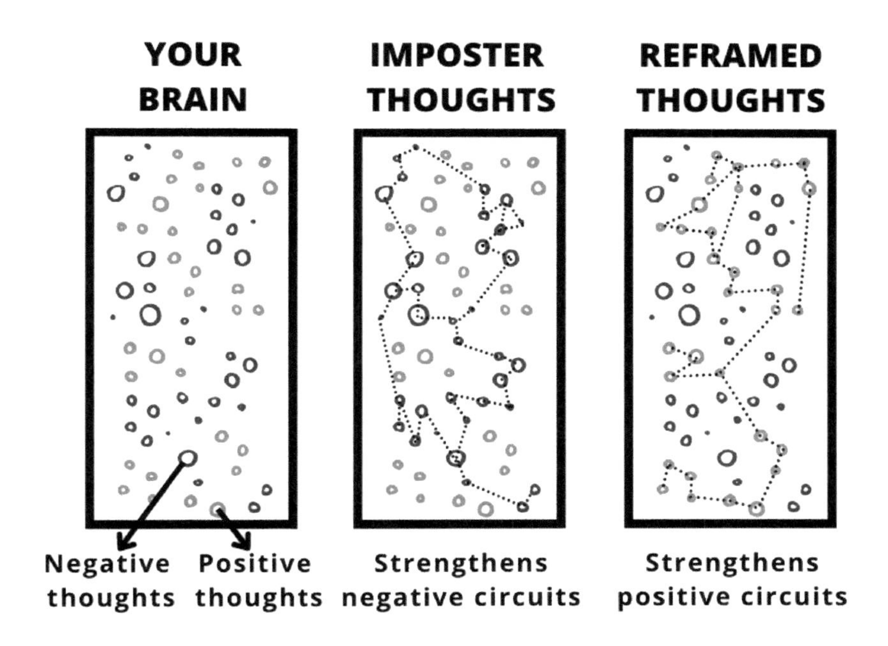

Here's the three-step process to rewire your brain:

1. Name it to tame it
2. Reframe your thoughts
3. Reinforce through action

Name it to tame it

You can't change what you don't notice. So, the first step in rewiring your brain is to start with self-awareness and catch your imposter thoughts as they arise in real-time. Instead of letting these thoughts slip through your consciousness, become fully aware of them as they show up. Also called mindfulness, Susan David, author of *Emotional Agility* says "Mindfulness guides us to become more emotionally agile by allowing us to observe the thinker having the thoughts. Simply paying attention brings the self out of the shadows. It creates the space between thought and action that we need to ensure we're acting with volition, rather than simply out of habit. But mindfulness is more than knowing 'I'm hearing something', or being aware 'I'm seeing something', or even noticing 'I'm having a feeling'. It's about doing all this with balance and equanimity, openness and curiosity, and without judgement. It also allows us to create new, fluid categories. As a result, the mental state of mindfulness lets us see the world through multiple perspectives, and go forward with higher levels of self-acceptance, tolerance and self-kindness."[7]

It will require you to be mindful of different moments in your life, observing and seeing things as they are happening. When imposter feelings strike, recognize the emotions you're feeling and invite them in as you did in Chapter 9 (Remember Buddha inviting Mara to tea). Do not judge them. Remind yourself that you have no control over their presence. All you need to do is be aware and step outside of your emotions without overthinking or overanalyzing or acting on them.

Next, name the emotion to tame the emotion. In other words, say to yourself, out loud, what negative emotion you're experiencing, as you're experiencing it. For example: when a negative emotion like fear comes with feeling like a fraud, say "I'm experiencing fear." Simply naming it is going to calm you down. This technique introduced by psychologist Dan Siegel[8] creates a bit of space between you and that emotion. Naming your emotions tends to diffuse their charge and lessen the burden they create.

There's another advantage of naming emotions this way. Matthew Lieberman is a Professor of Psychology at the University of California Los Angeles (UCLA). His research has shown that labeling of negative emotions, also called "affect labeling" can help people recover control.[9] His fMRI brain scan research shows that labeling of emotions decreases activity in the brain's emotional centers, including the amygdala. And once your amygdala is calm—that part of your brain involved in "fight-flight-freeze" mode—it gives you the chance to take a step back and come up with a more thoughtful response. Instead of letting your unconscious brain give in to your imposter thoughts and whatever emotion you experience as a result of it, recognizing and naming the emotion gives you a sense of control enabling you to choose a more appropriate response.

Reframe your thoughts

Naming the emotion and acknowledging it gives you just the space needed to address your imposter thoughts. Next, pay focused attention to the specific words you use to describe your feelings:

What are you saying to yourself?
What are the limiting beliefs you've been telling yourself?
What's the negative self-talk you're engaging in?

Then reframe these thoughts in a way that empowers you and shifts your negative self-talk from destructive to constructive. Reframing involves putting a different spin on your thoughts by looking at them from another perspective, one that involves a more helpful lens. Here are some of the ways to reframe your thoughts:

- Look for alternative ways to think about your situation.
- Involve problem-solving areas of your brain by asking questions that challenge your thinking.
- Use compassion to acknowledge that you're learning and evolving each day.
- Consider mistakes and failures as learning opportunities. Focus on progress as opposed to achieving specific outcomes (use learning goals discussed in chapter 10).
- Use past evidence in the form of your accomplishments, positive feedback, or comments to refute negative thoughts (use the evidence collected in chapter 11).

Use these reframing examples to shift your imposter thoughts from limiting you to empowering you.

SCENARIO	IMPOSTER THOUGHTS	REFRAME YOUR THOUGHTS
Taking on a new challenge	I'm going to fail terribly. It's better to opt out now.	What's the worst that can happen? What's the likelihood of it happening? If it does happen, how can I handle it?
You made a mistake	I suck at my job.	There are multiple times I have excelled at my job and received positive feedback. It's ok if I made a mistake

		this time. I can learn from this mistake and put measures in place that will help prevent it from happening again.
Considering a new opportunity	Everyone else is smart, intelligent, and competent. I don't have what it takes.	I am not alone in this experience. Others also feel this way. What can I learn from this opportunity? What new skills can I build?
When required to speak up	Others will find out how stupid and dumb are my thoughts.	I have made some really valuable suggestions in the past. There's no harm in sharing what I have to say.
When solving a complex problem	Procrastinate with the belief that nothing you do will be good enough.	How can I use my strengths to make it work? What other skills do I need?
When struggling with a task	If I were really smart, things would come easily to me.	I'm doing the best I can. It's normal for some things to be hard.
When required to ask for help	Others will find me incompetent.	Asking for help keeps me moving forward. I can learn new strategies and new

		ways of solving my problem.
You receive criticism	I am a failure and now others know too.	What does this feedback ask me to improve? How can I get better?
When trying to meet a deadline	They made a mistake in giving me this task. I can never meet this deadline. There's way too much to do.	Let me break it down into smaller tasks and see what I can do. I shall consider all the possibilities to make it work.
When networking	I should keep quiet to avoid being found out.	Meeting new people and sharing my perspective will help me build better connections.
Expected to deliver a project	It isn't perfect yet.	I will show this project to my boss and colleagues even though it isn't perfect to get their feedback.

Once you start reframing your thoughts, these new thoughts will become natural to you and your old thoughts that told you "you're not good enough" will wither away. Remember this though: your imposter thoughts may never completely go away. They may show up again within a different context or at a different time. Knowing these reframing strategies can help you deal with them as they arise.

Reinforce through action

You have named the emotion. You have reframed your thoughts. The final step to rewire your brain is to take action. It's the action that registers and makes the neural connections in your brain stronger. It changes the old thought patterns and replaces them with new powerful behaviors—behaviors that no longer block you from reaching your goals; behaviors that encourage you to take on a challenge; behaviors that consider mistakes and failures as learning lessons.

It's important that you start small. Small steps not only change your thinking over time, but they also turn off your brain's alarm system that resists and fears change. As Mark Twain, writer, humorist, and entrepreneur puts it "The secret of getting ahead is getting started. The secret of getting started is breaking your complex overwhelming tasks into smaller manageable tasks, and then starting on the first one."[10]

Consider these examples of small steps:

- Email your manager that you're excited about the new opportunity.
- Visualize asking for help in your mind.
- Write the first 5 lines of a draft proposal pending submission.
- Kick start the new skill by doing it only for 10 minutes.
- Practice sharing your opinions in a safe environment with your friends first.

John Wooden, the legendary basketball coach, also highlighted the importance of small improvements when he said "When you improve a little each day, eventually big things occur. When you improve conditioning a little each day, eventually you have a big improvement in conditioning. Not tomorrow, not the next day, but eventually a big gain is made. Don't look for the big, quick improvement. Seek small improvement one day at a time. That's the only way it happens—and when it happens, it lasts." These small steps may seem trivial at first, but they create new neural pathways through a series of small changes. Over a period of time, small consistent effort combines and turns into massive gains. You stop resisting these actions as the new connections in your brain makes them your default behaviors. They become a part of your being, something you desire on your own. You can't control your initial thoughts. But you can definitely control how you view them and the actions you take afterward. By naming your emotions, reframing negative self-talk, and taking small actions, you can turn down your inner critic which prevents you from going after the things you desire.

Let's do this exercise to rewire your brain and help you adopt new ways of thinking and acting.

Exercise: Reframe Negative Thinking

Do this activity anytime you experience imposter syndrome. When you first start, it's best to write it down. Over a period of time, you will notice that your brain is automatically trained to think this way. You can then follow this process in your mind instead of writing it down.

SITUATION	EMOTION	NEGATIVE SELF-TALK	REFRAMED THOUGHT	SMALL ACTION
What triggered your imposter feelings?	Which emotion did you feel?	What limiting belief did you tell yourself at this moment?	Reframe your thoughts using the strategies in this chapter	What small step can you take in the direction of this new thought?

You can download a printable version of "Reframe Negative Thinking" at:
techtello.com/rethink-imposter-syndrome/worksheets/

Your brain's natural fixation towards "bad" makes it give more weight to things that can go wrong than things that can go right. Combine that with your imposter feelings and it may seem impossible to achieve your long-term goals. However, knowing how your brain works and using reframing strategy can help you overcome its instinctual reactions which often have devastating effects and instead go after the progress you've made. Rewiring your brain to not become distraught by a single mishap, embracing new opportunities, and realizing that you have the power to choose your response even in the most difficult situations can have a massive impact on your growth and success. As Victor E. Frankl, a neurologist, psychologist, and Holocaust survivor puts it in his book *Man's Search for Meaning* "Between stimulus and response there is a space. In that space is our power to choose our response. In our response lies our growth and our freedom."[11]

While reframing helps to nudge your thoughts in the right direction, it's often not enough. Despite knowing what's the right thing to do, fear can get in the way. You may refuse to take on the opportunity or give up on the challenge assuming you are incompetent. But lack of competence is just an excuse you tell yourself to justify those feelings of discomfort. It's not competence, but your lack of self-confidence that gets in the way. In the next chapter, you'll learn to bridge this confidence gap through a series of tiny steps.

Chapter Summary

- Your brain is a series of circuits and pathways which is constantly learning and forming connections every moment. Every time you experience something and decide to act on it, it fires a pathway. When you do something consistently, the same pathway fires multiple times and strengthens the circuit.
- When you feel like a fraud and give in to those feelings by adopting self-sabotage behaviors, your brain learns to associate them together. Done multiple times, your brain switches to autopilot and makes these decisions for you. Without your conscious awareness, a feeling of self-doubt makes you give up new opportunities, avoid challenges, and only do work that feels safe.

- Your brain is not fixed. You can change its programming. You can teach your brain to think in new ways because it can be rewired. Instead of giving in to your feelings of unworthiness, adopting behaviors that are aligned with your goals and desires can shift your brain from destructive to constructive.
- Instead of trying to replace negative self-talk with positive affirmations, reframe your thoughts. Use self-compassion, alternative explanations, and the power of questions to engage in a conscious choice.
- The first step to rewire your brain is to name the emotion as you feel it. Naming it creates a distance between you and the emotion and gives you the space needed to choose a more thoughtful response. The next step is to reframe the thoughts by shifting the language you use to describe those emotions. Finally, taking an action aligned with the new thoughts creates the connection needed to repeat those behaviors.

CHAPTER 13

Step 5: Bridge the Confidence Gap

IMPOSTER SYNDROME may cause you to run around with excuses in your head, feel paralyzed with self-doubt, make it hard to muster up the courage to share your opinion, cause you to dwell on mistakes and failures, and play the negative tape in your mind on repeat. When you fall for its thinking traps, you may assume it's lack of competence that stops you from going after the things you want. But it's not competence that's holding you back, it's your lack of confidence. When you lose sight of belief in yourself, no amount of competence can make you successful. Competence gives you the skills, confidence underpins your ability to actually get things done.

Katty Kay and Claire Shipman, authors of the book *The Confidence Code* say "Success correlates more closely with confidence than it does with competence."[1] Research also shows that confidence is more important than ability when it comes to getting ahead. In a 1982 study, psychologists Barry Schlenker and Mark Leary explored this connection between confidence and perceptions of competence. A sample of 48 people was asked to rate the competence of 60 hypothetical individuals facing a tennis tournament. They received two pieces of information: their predicted performance from very poor to very good and their actual performance. After that, they had to rate each hypothetical individual's competence. Research concluded with this observation: those who made optimistic predictions of their match were perceived by the sample observers as more competent than those with more modest predictions, more so when their claim was in congruence with their performance or when the observers did not have data of their actual performance.[2] In effect, their confidence significantly influenced how others perceived their competence.

This doesn't mean you fake confidence when you know you won't perform well. Genuine confidence comes from having realistic evaluations of your skills and abilities without self-deprecation. The question stands: how can you do this when your mind is telling you just the opposite? When it's constantly asking you to downplay your achievements. When it's saying you don't belong. When it's asking you to give up before you have even begun? How can you be confident when you don't even believe you're competent?

We'll get to it. But first, let's define confidence.

Dr. Ivan Joseph, an award-winning performance coach who has coached national and world champions and Olympians defines confidence as “the ability or the belief to believe in yourself to accomplish any task, no matter the odds, no matter the difficulty, no matter the adversity. The belief that you can accomplish it.”[3] This is indeed one of the most common ways to describe confidence. In this definition, confidence is a feeling: a feeling that you can do well or succeed at something. But, there’s another definition of confidence that we often overlook. Derived from the Latin word 'fidere' which means "to trust," confidence is also defined as trust that a chosen course of action is the best or most effective.[4] Put this way, confidence is an action. It’s not a feeling of absolute certainty that you’ll achieve the outcome, an absence of fear from possible failures, or lack of self-doubt from what might possibly go wrong. Rather, the courage to act despite feeling those feelings; trusting yourself to take action no matter the end result. Put this way, confidence is not bailing at the first sign of failure, first challenge, or first encounter with adversity. Confidence is also persistence: the ability to get out there, do the work, and stick with it no matter the difficulty.

When you only think of confidence as a feeling, it can take you down a dark path conjuring up negative thoughts and coming up with all the reasons why you can't do something. By considering confidence as an action, your mind shifts to effective problem-solving instead of being stuck. It helps you come up with strategies to overcome obstacles, advises you on how to improve and build new skills, and what you can do to learn, grow and develop. Failures and mistakes are no longer disasters. Confidence in your ability to act helps you approach them in a constructive manner making you better prepared to deal with them when they arise.

This is what Russ Harris, an author and a leading authority on stress management calls "The Confidence Gap." He says people get stuck in it when they hold on to the belief that "I have to feel confident before I can achieve my goals, perform at my peak, do the things I want to do, or behave like the person I want to be."[5] When already dealing with feelings of unworthiness and self-doubt, if you wait to feel confident before you do what matters, you might have to wait for a very long time. Genuine confidence doesn't come from lack of fear. It's built by changing your relationship with fear or as Russ Harris puts it "The actions of confidence come first; the feelings of confidence come later."[6]

Russ demonstrates the power of taking action through his own struggles with confidence as a teenager in his twenties.[7] He was incredibly anxious in social situations, full of self-doubt, and terrified of coming across as dull, stupid, or unlikable. Long before he reached the legal drinking age, he started relying on alcohol to help him cope, and by the end of his first year at medical school, he was drinking heavily on a daily basis. This got progressively worse, and on one occasion, in his third year at medical school, he was admitted to hospital, via ambulance, with alcohol poisoning. His low self-confidence also played out in intimate relationships. He was so afraid of rejection that he never asked girls to go out with him unless he was drunk.

At medical school, he was convinced that he was more stupid than everyone else in his year. Whenever he tried to plow his way through all those thick, complex textbooks of anatomy, physiology, and biochemistry, all his self-doubt came gushing to the surface. So what did he do? He didn't like those feelings of anxiety, or those thoughts about being stupid, so to avoid them, he avoided studying! And the consequence? For the first two years at medical school, he failed every single exam and had to resit them all. After giving up on many things that were important to him due to lack of self-confidence, he was able to learn and change. He realized that confidence is a skill that can be cultivated. He wasn't born confident. But by working at it, he too was able to overcome his lack of self-confidence. Now Russ travels all over the world training coaches, psychologists, doctors, and other health professionals. He's also a consultant to the World Health Organization.

He says that instead of getting caught up in your thoughts and trying to fight them or evaluate if they're true or false, what matters more is whether they're helpful. To empower yourself to take action and be who you really want to be, even when your mind is generating all sorts of reasons as to why that can't happen, ask, if you allow these thoughts to guide your actions:

- Will they help you achieve the results you want?
- Will they help you to be the person you want to be?
- Will they help you to create the life you want to live?

If the answer is 'no', then you can recognize that the thought is 'unhelpful.' For Russ, confidence turned out to be a choice. It worked for him because he decided to take action to deal with his feelings of self-doubt instead of waiting for self-doubt to disappear before doing anything.

CREATE YOUR CONFIDENCE PLAN

Before you create a plan of action to gain confidence, let's get something out of the way. Do you tend to think in extremes? I'm either disciplined or I'm not. I'm either a good person or I'm not. I'm either brave or I'm not. I'm either pretty or I'm not. I'm either successful or I'm not. I'm either confident or I'm not. Can you see that when you think this way, there's no middle ground? This form of black-and-white thinking or all-or-nothing thinking is what leads to negative ruminations with low self-worth and feelings of self-doubt. When the two words in your dictionary "always" and "never" rule your life, it's hard to see mistakes and failures as one-off events and not a true measure of your worth. Placing everything into boxes of "good" and "bad" leaves no room for balanced perspectives.

- I can never do anything well.
- I am always such a failure.
- I am never going to succeed.
- I can never be as talented as him.

Instead of operating at the extremes, your life is somewhere in between. You're good at some things and bad at others. You fail at some things and succeed at others. You're confident about some skills and not so sure about others. Think about it for a moment, are you really not confident about anything you do? There are many things in life you might be good at. You can probably:

- Drive a car without thinking about crashing.
- Cook a fantastic meal without worrying about burning.
- Teach your kids to read and write without doubting your skills.
- Mow your lawn with perfect edges and trimmed grass with ease.
- Run ten miles a day without breaking a sweat.

You take them for granted because of how naturally they now seem to come to you. But did you not struggle with them when you first started? Were you confident about them even when you didn't have the skills? Did you have no feelings of self-doubt? You probably feared and doubted everything. Lack of experience and lack of skill when you first started would have led to many moments of struggle. You might have judged and criticized yourself or felt dissatisfied with slow progress. But, as you kept practicing them, after a while they stopped consuming your mental energy. What was once difficult turned natural. Soon all this competence which was a result of your effort and hard work turned into a routine. You don't realize that routine competence in so many things you do well is nothing but confidence.

You learned to read and write, ride a bike, swim and catch a ball as a kid. Then as an adult, you probably learned to drive, cook a meal, play sports, exercise, give a speech, lead a meeting or build other skills that are useful at work. You were able to do this up until now because your brain can learn new skills and behaviors at any age. So, back to the pertinent question: how do you build confidence? There's no magic trick to build confidence. You need to keep doing what you've been doing all along: by taking action, by doing the thing, by practicing. Every challenge you take on, and every new skill you build will take you closer to the life you deeply desire.

CONFIDENCE CYCLE

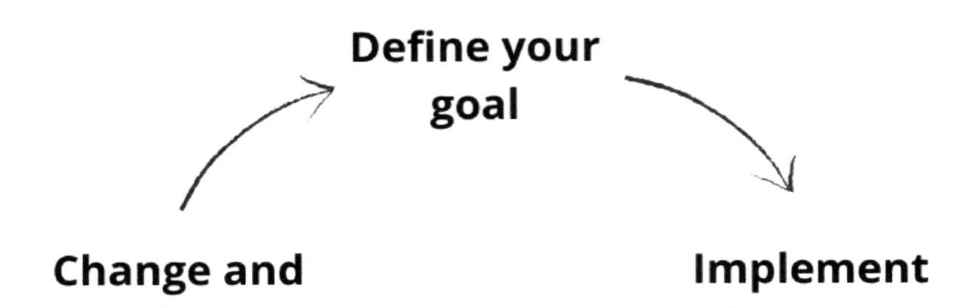

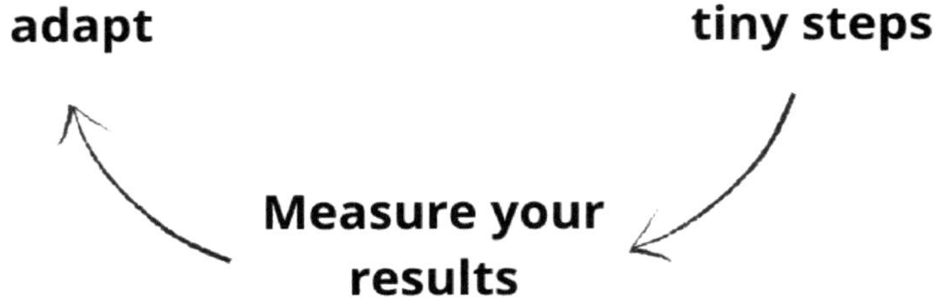

Now that you know that replacing your self-doubt with positive action is a great strategy to build confidence, follow this 3-step process:

1. Implement tiny steps
2. Measure your results
3. Change and adapt

Implement tiny steps

When taking on a new challenge, a new assignment, or doing something for the very first time, a wave of self-doubt is unavoidable. Thinking about the outcome or the end result can stop you from getting started. The sheer volume and complexity of the task combined with the possibility of a failure make it all the more harder. The path to reach your destination may not be clear yet, but you can get there through a series of tiny steps. Tiny steps require breaking down your goal into small, daily actions where each step takes you closer to the task.

For example:

- To give a presentation, practice speaking out loud in front of a mirror for a few days. Next, practice in front of a friend or a family member. Next, do it with your team. Keep increasing the challenge till you get to a point where giving a presentation seems natural.
- To write a book, start with writing 100 words daily. Increase the daily count from 100 to 200 to 500 to 1000 to 2000 gradually. Get feedback on your first draft from people you trust. Make edits. Repeat the process with others in your network.
- To negotiate a deal, practice negotiating in daily life with your kids, spouse, manager, or team members. Next, practice the actual deal using role play with a team member or someone who's known to be good at negotiating. Do this with multiple coworkers to get experience across varied negotiating styles.

Why are tiny steps useful? Tiny steps turn off your brain's alarm system that resists and fears change, keeps you engaged and focused on the task in the present, and leads to continual improvement—three essential components to build confidence. These small steps may seem trivial at first but practiced repeatedly they strengthen neural pathways in your brain which makes these small steps easier to perform. What was once daunting becomes second nature. The new connections in your brain create the thrill of the next challenge.

These tiny steps lead to small wins which Charles Duhigg, author of *The Power of Habit* describes as "Small wins are exactly what they sound like, and are part of how keystone habits create widespread changes. A huge body of research has shown that small wins have enormous power, an influence disproportionate to the accomplishments of the victories themselves...Once a small win has been accomplished, forces are set in motion that favor another small win. Small wins fuel transformative changes by leveraging tiny advantages into patterns that convince people that bigger achievements are within reach."[8]

Once you have the tiny steps identified, put them into action using what Peter Gollwitzer, psychologist, and researcher on how goals and plans affect cognition, emotion, and behavior, describes as creating implementation intentions—making a plan beforehand about when and where you intend to take action. In other words, when situation x arises, I will perform response y. Research shows that by simply writing down a plan that specifies exactly when and where you intend to engage in action, you are more likely to follow through.[9]

Implementation intention = I will [DO ACTION] at [TIME] in [LOCATION]

For example:

- I will write 100 words for my book from Monday to Saturday at 7 AM at my work desk.
- I will practice speaking the content of my presentation in front of a mirror at 8 PM every night after dinner in my bedroom.
- I will practice negotiating with my team members on Monday and Wednesday at 2 PM right after lunch in a conference room.

What if things don't go according to plan? Think about all the obstacles that might derail you from taking action and devise an alternative plan to deal with them. This will help you better prepare to adjust to unexpected events and stay on track no matter what comes your way. To do this, design implementation intentions using the "if-then" version.

If [THIS HAPPENS], then I will [DO THIS]

For example:

- If I cannot write 100 words for my book on Monday at 7 AM since I have to attend my son's school event, then I will do it Monday evening at 8 PM.
- If I cannot practice for my presentation at 8 PM on Thursday since it's my brother's birthday, then I will practice the next morning at 6 AM.
- If I cannot practice negotiation skills on Wednesday at 2 PM since there's an all-hands meeting at the same time, I will do it with my team at 6 PM after the meeting is over.

Breaking down your goals into tiny steps and acting on them using implementation intentions turns them into small wins. Small wins add up to major life goals. What once seemed out of your reach now fits perfectly within your comfort zone. Tiny steps strategy works for any opportunity you want to take on, any challenge you need to face, or any skill you want to master.

Measure your results

Peter Drucker, management guru said, "What's measured improves."[10] This is true for everything in life. Whether you are trying to accomplish a goal, build a new skill, or work on a difficult task, without the attitude to learn, adapt and make corrections along the way, you cannot improve. A great way to do this is to implement a strong feedback loop in your process.

Measure how you're doing every day without judgment—without beating yourself up. When you don't measure up to your own expectations, don't engage in ruthless self-criticism as it will discourage improvement. Self-criticism can often backfire by increasing your unhappiness levels and make you procrastinate instead of putting in the effort to achieve your goals. Instead reflect on the results by thinking about the actions you can take:

- What worked well?
- What didn't work? How can you do it differently next time around?
- What obstacles did you not foresee?
- What feedback do you have from others based on the progress you've made?
- What changes do your tiny steps need based on everything you have learned so far?

Change and adapt

Finally, nothing good can come out of all this effort if you aren't willing to change and adapt. You've implemented a few tiny steps. You've measured your results. Now, don't back out and delay making changes to your process, even if they seem hard at first. It's also important that you tweak and adapt to changes around you instead of being inflexible. Look for the signals in your environment. Does something seem off?

For example: Let's imagine you have been tasked with the responsibility to roll out a new process in your organization. You have finalized a strategy based on data and feedback collected from your team and other functions. You test launch a small part of this strategy with high hopes. But wait, it fails astonishingly. While measuring your results, you discover a key assumption that's no longer valid. You know what this means. You have to go back to the drawing board and redo the homework. Your mind by this time would have already started playing its self-defeating story "You're no good" "You screwed up. Everyone is going to find out you're a fraud."

That's just your mind. It's doing its work. You need to do yours. Take a moment and think about it, what's better: sticking to a plan that clearly does not work or pulling up your socks and getting back to work? Recognize that you identified a wrong assumption before rolling out the entire strategy. Acknowledge your knowledge and skills that helped you save so much time and effort. Celebrate that it's not too late. Reframe this minor setback from thinking "I failed" to "I now know for sure what doesn't work." Come up with a new strategy and repeat the process: implement tiny changes, measure your results, and change and adapt.

Following this three-step process and paying attention to your progress is the perfect antidote to your feelings of unworthiness and self-doubt. You can see for yourself that everything your mind tells you isn't true. You have proof: you have taken action. You have learnt. You have made tremendous progress. None of this was possible if you simply believed your judgmental thoughts and decided to do nothing. Confidence comes from getting past your fears by doing the work, not from doing nothing.

Let's do this exercise to bridge the confidence gap.

Exercise: Bridge the Confidence Gap

Consider any opportunity you want to embrace or a goal or task that you want to accomplish. If you've been putting it off due to fear of failure or risk of not meeting expectations, do it anyway. Follow the steps below to build confidence through action.

Step 1: Shift from thoughts to action

Instead of waiting to feel confident before doing the thing, tell yourself "The actions of confidence come first; the feelings of confidence come later." Write this on a piece of paper in bold and stick it near your area of work.

Repeating "action is more important than feeling" will put you in the right frame of mind and get you prepped up to take action.

Step 2: Put your goal in writing

Write down in a few lines what exactly you wish to accomplish. Stating your goal clearly will help you measure your progress later.

____

____

Step 3: Break it into tiny steps

Try to think about the small steps you can take to accomplish this goal or task. You don't have to break down every single step on day 1. Instead of trying to be perfect, just start somewhere. As you progress, keep revising your plan to include new steps.

STEPS	STATE YOUR INTENTION TO ACT	WHEN IT DOES NOT GO ACCORDING TO PLAN
Write down each step	I will [DO ACTION] at [TIME] in [LOCATION]	If [THIS HAPPENS], then I will [DO THIS]

Step 4: Measure your results

Setup periodic checkpoints to measure your progress. Write down your answer to these questions:

1. What worked well?

____

____

2. What didn't work? How can you do it differently next time around?

____

____

3. What obstacles did you not foresee?

____

____

4. What feedback do you have from others based on the progress you've made?

____

____

5. What changes do your tiny steps need based on everything you have learnt so far?

____

____

Step 5: Change and adapt

Based on your learnings from step 4, put required changes into action. Incorporate them into your plan and repeat the process starting with step 3.

Every time you make a change, keep a log of that change with reasoning on why you made that decision. This will help you evaluate your changes later to separate good from bad decisions.

CHANGES TO PLAN	DATE/TIME	REASON

You can download a printable version of "Bridge the Confidence Gap" at:
techtello.com/rethink-imposter-syndrome/worksheets/

This poem from P. Bodi, an author and a poet sums up confidence beautifully:

Feeling out of place,
Like you don't belong,
Like others will find out
You've been 'faking it'
All along,
But confidence is not a
Given, it is grown, keep

Building it, step by step,
Until it is your own.
— P. Bodi[11]

Human beings are wired to compare. More often than not what gets their attention are the things they see in others that they want in themselves. Negative feelings that come from obsessing about your flaws and imperfections make comparison a zero-sum game. Instead of comparing yourself to others, invest in gaining self-mastery by comparing yourself to your own ideal self. In the next chapter, you'll learn strategies to become the best version of yourself even when accompanied by feelings of inadequacy and self-doubt.

Chapter Summary

- Imposter syndrome can make you attribute your feelings of inadequacy and self-doubt to lack of competence. But, you don't lack competence. What you need is self-confidence.
- If you wait to feel completely confident before taking on any new opportunity or a challenge, you'll need to wait for a long time. Instead build confidence by taking action, doing the thing first.
- Confidence is often linked with a feeling, a belief that you can accomplish anything that your heart desires. But there's another side of confidence that's more useful when dealing with feelings of self-doubt. In this definition, confidence is action: the trust you place in a certain decision, the steps you take to get past obstacles through effective problem-solving, and the persistence to stay with a specific course of action.

- Instead of viewing confidence with the lens of all-or-nothing thinking—you either have it or you don't—look for a more balanced perspective. There are a lot of things you do well in life. These are the skills you did not possess when you first started. You don't consider them as confidence because of how natural they feel now.
- Much like anything in life, confidence can be acquired. To do it, follow this process: break down any goal you wish to accomplish into tiny steps, measure your results and change and adapt.

CHAPTER 14

Step 6: Start Competing With Self

DO YOU COMPARE yourself to others? Do you wish you could do what they're capable of doing? Do you ruminate about the things you don't have—intelligence, confidence, presence—and feel inadequate when you see it in others? While comparison is naturally tempting and can sometimes be a valuable source of motivation and growth, not considering the downsides of using others as a benchmark of your worth can trap you within a frenzy of constant self-doubt. Playing the comparison game can lead to feelings of inadequacy if the rate at which you're achieving things doesn't measure up in comparison to others' bigger and better accomplishments.

But why do you compare even when you don't have the same goals, circumstances, or even the same opportunities as others? According to the social comparison theory proposed by psychologist Leon Festinger,[1] you do it in an attempt to make an accurate evaluation of yourself. Comparing your attitudes, abilities, and traits to others helps you know yourself better—areas you're doing well and where you are lacking. The problem is not with the comparison itself, but how you view it: do you recognize it as a tool to make yourself better or is it just a yardstick to make you feel less worthy?

For example...

- When someone produces high-quality work, do you use it as an inspiration to do better or does it reinforce your self-limiting belief that you can never do as well as them irrespective of how hard you try?
- When someone gets a promotion, are you driven to achieve more and improve your abilities or does their promotion make you envious with the belief you don't have what it takes?
- When someone learns a new skill you're struggling to build, do you consider it as an opportunity to learn from them, or does the comparison highlight your inadequacies, making you believe you're good for nothing?

Comparing yourself to someone who has achieved something, or someone who's more successful than you is one thing, but what if instead of looking upward to people who are doing better than you, you look downward to those who are doing worse to feel better about yourself? According to psychologist Juliana Breines, we make downward comparisons when our self-esteem is threatened—for example, if we've just received negative feedback—because these comparisons give us a boost, enhance our own perceived standing, and reassure us that things could be worse. She explains that even though downward comparisons may seem harmless, even healthy, they have several drawbacks "First, to the extent that these comparisons form a basis for self-esteem, it's a fragile one because they depend on the continued misfortune of others. Downward comparison can also put a strain on our relationships. When we focus too narrowly on others' negative attributes, we may miss the complete picture of their strengths and successes, which limits our ability to empathize and support them in good times and bad."

UPWARD

CONTRASTING WITH UPWARD TARGET

Feelings of frustration, shame and resentment

IDENTIFYING WITH UPWARD TARGET

Optimistic with feelings of admiration and inspiration

CONTRAST

IDENTIFY

CONTRASTING WITH DOWNWARD TARGET

Feelings of competition and jealousy

IDENTIFYING WITH DOWNWARD TARGET

Feelings of fear and worry

DOWNWARD

When you engage in social comparison, either by looking upward to someone who's doing better than you or downward to someone who is doing worse, it can have a positive or negative effect on your motivation and mood. That's because the positive or negative quality of the emotions that come from social comparison results from two factors:[3]

1. Whether the comparison is upward or downward.
2. Position that you take in relation to your target. When you perceive yourself to be similar to the target, you adopt a position of identification; when you consider yourself to be different from the target, you adopt a position of contrast.

This creates four possible types of social comparisons:[4]

Identifying with an upward target: makes you more optimistic and leads to feelings of admiration and inspiration.

Contrasting with an upward target: leads to feelings of frustration, low self-confidence, shame, resentment, and envy.

Identifying with a downward target: can lead to feelings of fear—you might worry that you'll get results as poor as your comparison target.

Contrasting with a downward target: can make you feel happy and proud momentarily, but focusing on other people's misfortunes in order to feel adequate only fuels feelings of competitiveness and jealousy in the long run.

How does social comparison play out when you're accompanied by imposter feelings? When you feel like an imposter, your self-evaluation is colored by a negative bias. This makes you seek and retain information that validates your feelings of inadequacy. You identify with people who are less successful (downward target) and contrast yourself with those who are more successful (upward target). Downward identification perpetuates the belief that others overestimate your skills and abilities while upward contrast reminds you that you do not belong with others who are more talented.[5] Ruminating about how others are more talented, more skilled, and more intelligent than you is not only time-consuming, the unconscious realization that you can never be as good as them can be self-destructive. It can eat away into your time and energy that's better spent in fulfilling your goals.

Oliver Burkeman, a journalist and a writer says "One of the biggest causes of misery is the way we chronically compare our insides with other people's outsides. We're all mini-New York Timeses or White Houses, energetically projecting an image of calm proficiency, while inside we're improvising in a mad panic. Yet we forget (especially in an era of carefully curated Facebook profiles and suchlike) that everyone else is doing the same thing. The only difference is that they think it's you who's truly competent."[6] Steven Furtick, pastor, author, and award-winning songwriter echoes the idea "The reason we struggle with insecurity is because we compare our behind-the-scenes with everyone else's highlight reel."

Instead of beating yourself up with the accomplishments of those around you, what if you compared yourself to your own ideal self—the person you wish to become? When life is about becoming a better version of yourself, you're no longer concerned with falling short in comparison to others. Rather, what matters is how you're improving, what you're learning, and whether you're getting better each day. This fundamental shift is what Warren Buffet, one of the most successful investors in the world and CEO of Berkshire Hathaway refers to as keeping an "inner scorecard." The inner scorecard refers to living through values that are important to you. The outer scorecard refers to what could be measured by those around you.[7]

Mike Krzyzewski, a Naismith Hall of Fame coach, a five-time national champion at Duke, and a six-time gold medalist as head Coach of the US Men's National Team gave this advice to every player when they came to Duke "Each of you run your own individual race...Don't gauge yourself with what another kid is doing. Gauge yourself on how you're doing." He gives examples of Elton Brand and Shane Battier who came in on the same year. Shane Battier was the National high school player of the year while Elton Brand was McDonald's All-American ranked 18th. By the end of his sophomore year, Elton Brand was the National Player of the Year and the number-one draft pick in the NBA. If Shane Battier was running Elton Brand's race, he'd be disappointed. Shane had a different race to run—two years later he was the National Player of the Year and the sixth pick in the NBA Draft.[8] Shane did not let someone else's scorecard derail him from his path. He used his inner scorecard to raise himself up—by focusing his energy on what he was learning and how he was improving.

To remove unwanted feelings of ineptness and unworthiness that comes from social comparison, you need to start living with an inner scorecard. Using comparison to evaluate your worth is a lost battle. Instead of lamenting about your flaws, redirect your energy towards becoming the best version of yourself. Instead of using someone else to define your self-worth, consider yourself worthy of your goals and do the work required to achieve them.

To do this, identify:

- What matters to you?
- What relationships do you want to have?
- What experiences are the most important to you?
- How do you envision your life?

Thinking about what matters to you is hard. Measuring yourself against what you want your life to be about may not be fun. But, it's the only way to live a free life—free from those nagging feelings of ineptness and self-doubt. Whenever you find yourself slipping into comparison, intentionally shift from comparing yourself to others to comparing yourself to your past self—how have you grown, what have you learnt, how much have you focused on your own goals, and what is required to achieve them? Moving at your own pace makes you feel in control; setting your own expectations gives you the freedom to make decisions aligned with your goals. There's another advantage to thinking this way: no one can beat you in a game of life that requires being you. You're the only person who can do it best.

Embracing this new way of life does not mean setting low expectations for yourself or doing work that feels comfortable. It's not about laying low, but rather rising up to new challenges; it requires taking several steps outside your comfort zone. When you're building new skills, pushing through the discomfort, or coming face-to-face with your mistakes, those negative feelings of self-doubt are bound to strike again. In those moments of struggle, recalibrate your internal voice from being critical and judgmental to one that is forgiving and understanding.

MAKE SPACE FOR SELF-COMPASSION

When you're feeling inadequate, what is it that you crave the most? A good dose of self-esteem? However, trying to build your self-esteem does what it's good at—disregarding, rationalizing, or sweeping the issue under the rug. Dodging off responsibility for your failures, blaming others for how things turned out, or simply hoping the problem to vanish like a puff of smoke will not make it disappear. The problem will soon explode in your face causing more damage than good. When these self-esteem boosting strategies don't work, what do you do next?

You may turn to self-criticism: with the hope that it will motivate you to do better. When you're already feeling insecure, berating yourself about your inadequacies only demotivates you further. It's the good old carrot-and-stick approach that clearly does not work or

You may look downward: to other people who aren't doing so well. Trying to feel better by raising your status makes you fall right back into the trap of social comparison.

Self-esteem, once the ultimate mark of positive mental health, is no longer the gold standard to achieve better performance or greater success. Roy Baumeister, a social psychologist who explores how we think about the self, and why we feel and act the way we do along with other psychologists established that boosting self-esteem does not lead to improved outcomes, increase your job performance, make you a more effective leader, a better partner, or encourage you to choose healthy lifestyle options. High self-esteem is the consequence rather than being the cause of those healthy behaviors.[9]

SELF-COMPASSION

Being kind, gentle, and accepting of yourself brings growth

SELF-CRITICISM

Resistance, denial, anger and frustration compounds suffering

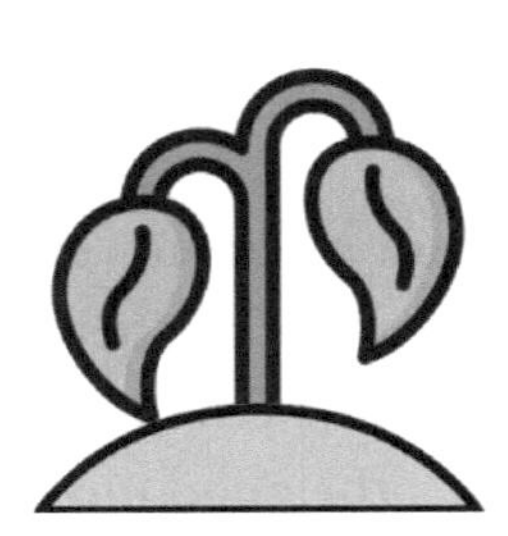

Instead of grasping onto self-esteem when you mess up or things go wrong, Kristin Neff, a pioneer in self-compassion study suggests another path—one in which you stop judging and evaluating yourself altogether. Where you don't need to label yourself as "good" or "bad" and simply accept yourself with an open heart. This path she suggests leads to self-compassion "Instead of mercilessly judging and criticizing yourself for various inadequacies or shortcomings, self-compassion means you are kind and understanding when confronted with personal failings. Instead of just ignoring your pain with a "stiff upper lip" mentality, you stop to tell yourself "this is really difficult right now," how can I comfort and care for myself in this moment?"[10]

Self-compassion is the ability to face your mistakes and failures with kindness and understanding without letting them define you or determine your worthiness. It's having the same sense of warmth, empathy, and positive regard for yourself as you would have for another person when they are dealing with a difficult circumstance. For example, if a friend approaches you and tells you how they screwed up the other day and now feel completely unworthy of their position, would you not comfort and reassure them, remind them of how smart and capable they are, and explain that mistakes are a natural part of learning and growth? Self-compassion is giving yourself the same reassurance whenever you fail or feel inadequate: "Mistakes don't define me. I can learn from this mistake. I can implement a new strategy and try again."

Self-compassion is the perfect antidote to imposter feelings:

- It is strongly associated with emotional resilience and psychological well-being.[11]
- It can curb the avoidance tendencies that arise with imposter syndrome.[12]
- People who are self-compassionate have lower levels of depression and anxiety, are less likely to ruminate on negative thoughts and emotions or suppress them, show increased optimism, are able to take personal initiative, and are

involved with more positive emotions like kindness, happiness, and connectedness.[13]

Instead of hiding from challenges or beating yourself up when you feel inadequate, self-compassion gives you the resilience to learn from your mistakes. It helps you normalize negative feelings by acknowledging that discomfort is a natural part of human experience. It also enables you to move on when faced with setbacks instead of getting stuck in endless rumination about what went wrong. Viewing yourself with the lens of self-compassion makes fear of failure no longer a reflection of your incompetence, but rather part of shared experience.

3 COMPONENTS OF SELF-COMPASSION

To make self-compassion a part of your life, put these three essential components into practice:[14]

1. Self-kindness
2. Common humanity
3. Mindfulness

Self-kindness

Irrespective of how much effort you put into something or how hard you try, you will never succeed at everything—external circumstances might get in the way, your strategy may fall through, or an unexpected turn of events may sabotage your plan. With self-judgment, difficult moments, personal shortcomings, failures, and mistakes that are inevitable aspects of life are met with resistance, denial, anger, frustration, and criticism. Fighting this reality further compounds the suffering making it much harder to deal with your struggles when they arise.

A self-compassionate view requires accepting your pain, suffering, and feelings of inadequacy with sympathy, kindness, and understanding. It requires not engaging in self-criticism when confronted with a personal failing. Rather, being kind, gentle, and accepting of yourself as a human being with imperfections and flaws. The warmth that ensues can turn anxiety into calmness, fear into trust, and insecurity into confidence.

Shift from self-criticism to self-kindness by using these examples...

SCENARIO	INSTEAD OF SELF-CRITICISM	SHIFT TO SELF-KINDNESS
When you make a mistake	Here I go again. I blew it. Why do I always do this? Seems like I'll never succeed!	I made a mistake and that's fine. I'm doing the best I can at this moment and that's enough.
When someone criticizes you	They're absolutely right. I am incompetent. I don't deserve anything.	I accept the best and worst aspects of who I am and not let judgment hold me back from the future I desire.
When learning something new	Why aren't I getting this? I'm no good and will never learn anything.	Learning something new is challenging. Some things I'm able to catch on quickly and some slower. That's ok. If I stick with it long enough, I'll get it.
When things don't go as expected	This was bound to happen. I'm useless. Nothing I do works out.	Not everything I do can turn out the way I'd like. The important thing is that I am learning and improving.

Kristin Neff puts it best "Instead of seeing ourselves as a problem to be fixed, therefore, self-kindness allows us to see ourselves as valuable human beings who are worthy of care. Self-kindness allows us to feel safe as we respond to painful experiences, so that we are no longer operating from a place of fear—and once we let go of insecurity we can pursue our dreams with the confidence needed to actually achieve them."[15]

Common humanity

When someone makes a mistake, the most common response is "It's only human." That's because all human beings are imperfect. Absorbed in your own feelings of insecurity, you may fail to realize that your feelings of inadequacy are nothing special, they're part of shared human experience. Once trapped inside a vicious cycle of unworthiness, you feel disconnected and isolated from the rest of humanity—the more inept, inadequate, and unworthy you feel, the stronger are your feelings that you don't belong.

For example...

- When you fail, it may appear that you're the only one who's having a hard time while everyone else around you seems to be doing pretty well.
- When you fear a challenge, it may appear that you're the only one who's uncertain while everyone else is beaming with self-confidence.
- When you doubt your skills and abilities to do well, it may appear that you're the only one feeling incompetent while everyone else is smart, intelligent, and capable who never doubts themselves.

Kristin Neff calls it the emotional tunnel vision. She suggests shifting from feeling isolated and alone to recognizing the interconnected nature of our lives "When we're in touch with our common humanity, we remember that feelings of inadequacy and disappointment are shared by all. This is what distinguishes self-compassion from self-pity. Whereas self-pity says "poor me," self-compassion remembers that everyone suffers, and it offers comfort because everyone is human. The pain I feel in difficult times is the same pain that you feel in difficult times. The triggers are different, the circumstances are different, the degree of pain is different, but the process is the same."[16]

When you make a mistake, face a challenge or worry about not having the skills and abilities to do well in life, practice self-compassion by recognizing that your feelings are part of being human. Tell yourself:

COMMON HUMANITY STATEMENTS
Nobody is perfect or immune from thinking the occasional fearful, irrational, or defensive thought.
Everybody feels self-doubt at some point or another.
Most people find themselves feeling this way in situations like this.
I'm not perfect and neither is anyone else.
I am not the only one finding this hard. Many others will find it hard too.
Everyone makes mistakes from time to time.
I am struggling today like so many people. And that's fine.

Mindfulness

A common reaction to tough emotions is suppression or exaggeration. Denying or suppressing your emotions does not make them disappear. Exaggeration is equally bad—over-identifying with your thoughts and feelings and getting caught up in them takes away your ability to connect with your emotions with openness and clarity.

When you fear failure, worry about falling short of meeting other people's expectations, or when you doubt your own skills and abilities, your mind gets so busy reminding you of your flaws and imperfections that you fail to approach your emotions with curiosity. Kristin Neff explains it this way "Our sense of self becomes so wrapped up in our emotional reactions that our entire reality is consumed by them. There's no mental space left over to say, "Gosh, I'm getting a bit worked up here. Maybe there's another way to look at this." Rather than stepping back and objectively observing what's occurring, we're lost in the thick of it. What we think and feel seems like a direct perception of reality, and we forget that we are putting a personal spin on things."[17]

Instead of operating at the extremes—suppressing the emotion or exaggerating it—mindfulness requires a balanced approach. It requires that you keep your judgments aside and become fully aware of what's occurring in the present moment—seeing things as they're so that you can respond to them in the most effective manner. Kristin writes "Mindfulness brings us back to the present moment and provides the type of balanced awareness that forms the foundation of self-compassion. Like a clear, still pool without ripples, mindfulness perfectly mirrors what's occurring without distortion. Rather than becoming lost in our own personal soap opera, mindfulness allows us to view our situation with greater perspective and helps to ensure that we don't suffer unnecessarily."[18]

To practice mindfulness, take a mental note of the particular thought, emotion, or sensation as it arises and become consciously aware of how you're feeling. Being fully engaged in the present will give you the perspective needed to deal with your emotions constructively. For example, when feelings of self-doubt, ineptness, or unworthiness arise, take a mental note of your thoughts and emotions: I am aware that I am feeling ______ in this moment. Being engaged with your feelings in this manner gives you the opportunity to respond to them effectively instead of reacting to them with harmful behaviors and actions.

Practicing these three core components of self-compassion—self-kindness, common humanity, and mindfulness—will require some work initially. But as you keep doing them, they will turn into a habit. You'll automatically be compassionate towards yourself when faced with imposter feelings.

Let's do this exercise to measure how self-compassionate you are, followed by the link to guided practices and exercises to cultivate self-compassion.

Exercise: Practice Self-Compassion

Let's first identify how self-compassionate you are. Read each of the statements below and indicate how often you behave in the stated manner using a 5-point scale (1 - Almost never, 2 - Occasionally, 3 - About half of the time, 4 - Fairly often, and 5 - Almost always). This exercise is developed by Kristin Neff.[19]

No.	STATEMENT	1	2	3	4	5
1	I'm disapproving and judgmental about my own flaws and					

	inadequacies.					
2	When I'm feeling down I tend to obsess and fixate on everything that's wrong.					
3	When things are going badly for me, I see the difficulties as part of life that everyone goes through.					
4	When I think about my inadequacies, it tends to make me feel more separate and cut off from the rest of the world.					
5	I try to be loving towards myself when I'm feeling emotional pain.					
6	When I fail at something important to me I become consumed by feelings of inadequacy.					
7	When I'm down and out, I remind myself that there are lots of other people in the world feeling like I am.					
8	When times are really difficult, I tend to be tough on myself.					
9	When something upsets me I try to keep my emotions in balance.					
10	When I feel inadequate in some way,					

	I try to remind myself that feelings of inadequacy are shared by most people.					
11	I'm intolerant and impatient towards those aspects of my personality I don't like.					
12	When I'm going through a very hard time, I give myself the caring and tenderness I need.					
13	When I'm feeling down, I tend to feel like most other people are probably happier than I am.					
14	When something painful happens I try to take a balanced view of the situation.					
15	I try to see my failings as part of the human condition.					
16	When I see aspects of myself that I don't like, I get down on myself.					
17	When I fail at something important to me I try to keep things in perspective.					
18	When I'm really struggling, I tend to feel like other people must be having an easier time of it.					

19	I'm kind to myself when I'm experiencing suffering.					
20	When something upsets me I get carried away with my feelings.					
21	I can be a bit cold-hearted towards myself when I'm experiencing suffering.					
22	When I'm feeling down I try to approach my feelings with curiosity and openness.					
23	I'm tolerant of my own flaws and inadequacies.					
24	When something painful happens I tend to blow the incident out of proportion.					
25	When I fail at something that's important to me, I tend to feel alone in my failure.					
26	I try to be understanding and patient towards those aspects of my personality I don't like.					

Use this coding key to calculate the total compassion score:
Self-Kindness Items: 5, 12, 19, 23, 26

Self-Judgment Items: 1, 8, 11, 16, 21
Common Humanity Items: 3, 7, 10, 15
Isolation Items: 4, 13, 18, 25
Mindfulness Items: 9, 14, 17, 22
Over-identified Items: 2, 6, 20, 24

Self-judgment is the opposite of self-kindness, isolation opposite of common humanity and over-identification opposite of mindfulness. Higher scores for self-judgment, isolation, and over-identification items indicate less self-compassion. To take this into account, reverse the scores of these items in the table above (1 = 5, 2 = 4, 3 = 3, 4 = 2, 5 = 1). For instance, the statement "When times are really difficult, I tend to be tough on myself" is related to self-judgment. A response of "almost always" should be reversed and scored as 1 rather than 5 when calculating an overall compassion score.

To compute your self-compassion score, calculate the total mean of all the responses above (don't forget to reverse the scores for self-judgment, isolation, and over-identification items).

My total self-compassion score is ___________

Use the table below to interpret your score.

SCORE 1-2.5	SCORE 2.5-3.5	SCORE 3.5-5.0
Low self-compassion	Moderate self-compassion	High self-compassion

Now that you know how self-compassionate you are, follow the guided practices and exercises to build self-compassion provided by Kristin Neff on her website self-compassion.org.

You can download a printable version of "Practice Self-Compassion" at:
techtello.com/rethink-imposter-syndrome/worksheets/

When faced with challenging circumstances or setbacks or when dealing with fear and self-doubt, shifting from punitive self-judgment to self-compassion creates the space necessary to take a step back and respond to your feelings with kindness. A compassionate view allows you to take a balanced perspective without getting caught up in your thoughts and feelings. Knowing that your feelings of self-doubt and inadequacy are not personal but part of a shared experience also gives you the confidence to move ahead—you feel calm and stable to take effective action. Elisabeth Kubler-Ross, a psychiatrist, and author writes "People are like stained-glass windows. They sparkle and shine when the sun is out, but when the darkness sets in, their true beauty is revealed only if there is a light from within." Self-compassion is that light that helps you shine even on your dark days.[20]

When you put these strategies into practice, you may not succeed at the first attempt. Don't give up—keep practicing them over and over again. Replace old ways of handling imposter thoughts with new behaviors and actions. Monitor your progress, observe your mistakes and make corrections. Repeating them often will align your brain to accept these new behaviors as default responses to your feelings of inadequacy and low self-worth. How to do it right? You'll find out in the next chapter.

Chapter Summary

- Comparison is a natural part of being human. You compare yourself to others to see how well you're doing.
- While comparing to others, you may either look upward to those who are doing better than you're or downward to those who are doing worse. Identifying upwards gives you the motivation to do well while contrasting with them leads to low self-worth. Similarly, identifying downwards creates the fear that you'll never succeed while contrasting downwards only raises your self-esteem without doing anything to help you achieve your goals.
- Feeling like an imposter highlights the negative aspects of comparison—you identify downwards and contrast upwards both of which perpetuates self-limiting beliefs.
- Instead of comparing to others, start competing with yourself. Try to attain self-mastery by becoming your own best version—identify what you're learning and how you're improving. In other words, shift from keeping an outer scorecard to building an inner scorecard.
- Competing with yourself is hard. It requires embracing new challenges and stepping outside your comfort zone. When doing that, your feelings of self-doubt are bound to strike again. Your natural instinct might be to raise your self-esteem to feel better about yourself. Don't.
- When feeling inadequate, instead of trying to build your self-esteem, practice self-compassion—be mindful by keeping a balanced perspective of your emotions, comfort yourself with kindness, and remind yourself that your experience is not unique and everyone struggles with such feelings from time to time.

CHAPTER 15

Step 7: Make It Last

THIS IS THE END of the book and beginning of a new journey for you. Creating space for this new way of thinking in your life requires practice. Once you start embracing all the strategies in this book and incorporate them into your daily life, it will take some time for your brain to adapt to these changes. Give it that space—let it make mistakes. Don't beat yourself up when you fall back to your old behaviors and attitudes, practice compassion—staying kind in those moments will give you just the perspective you need to move ahead with clarity and understanding.

Remind yourself:

- I am learning.
- I am getting better.
- It's okay to make mistakes.

The fact that you have come this far tells me that you're serious about this change. But, let me be honest, it's going to require hard work, patience, and persistence. Instead of trying to disrupt yourself with a big move and feeling frustrated when it doesn't happen, target incremental progress. For example, if perfectionism was your thing to deal with imposter feelings, it's unlikely you'll stop being a perfectionist right away. Years of training can't be washed away in a single day. Warren Buffet, chairman and CEO of Berkshire Hathaway said, "Chains of habit are too light to be felt until they are too heavy to be broken." Build your way up through small changes by focusing on the momentum. Slowly and carefully sow the seeds of change. Take small steps, measure your progress, adapt and repeat.

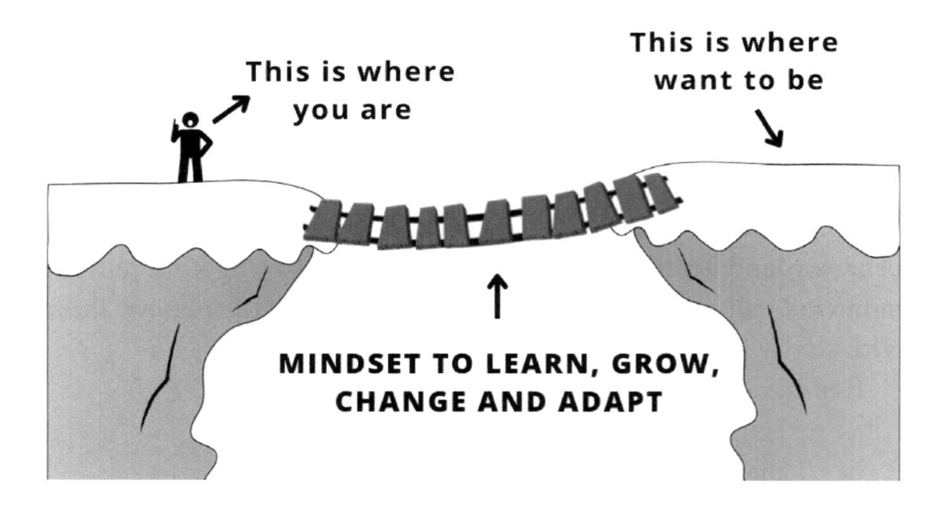

One belief that can often get in the way of a meaningful change is the mindset "This is who I am." When you believe that your personality is fixed and no amount of effort can change it, you already accept defeat. Carol Dweck, a Stanford psychologist calls it a fixed mindset. As I explain in my book *Upgrade Your Mindset*, a person with a fixed mindset believes that people are born with special talents and every person has different abilities and intelligence that cannot get better with time, effort, and determination. A growth mindset person on the other hand understands that certain people have special talents and that intelligence varies from person to person, but it's also something that can be developed and increased with effort and hard work.[1] Your personality is nothing but a result of this mindset. Fixed mindset prevents you from fulfilling your potential by making you believe that you can't change over time. Growth mindset on the other hand keeps you learning and growing by giving you the power to shape yourself into the person you wish to become. Research from Carol Dweck and multiple other psychologists has shown that even our deepest psychological traits can change over time with deliberate interventions.[2] With effort and perseverance, you're no longer limited by who you're; you can grow into the person you wish to become.

Consider these key differences between a fixed mindset and a growth mindset person:

FIXED MINDSET	GROWTH MINDSET
Believe their abilities cannot be developed	Believe in growing their abilities
Avoid new opportunities with fear of failure	Embrace new opportunities to master new skills
Worry about how they will be judged	Think about what they can learn
Give up when the going gets	Persevere in the face of failures

tough	and setbacks
Negative feedback impacts their self-worth	Accept criticism as a way to learn
Feel threatened when others succeed	Find inspiration in others' success
Consider mistakes as a reflection of their limitations	Consider mistakes as an opportunity to learn
Focus on raising self-esteem	Practice self-compassion

All those feelings of self-doubt and inadequacy did not appear one day out of the blue but are the product of your mindset—whether you view personality and intelligence as fixed or changeable. New opportunities and challenges are bound to scare the hell out of you when you believe that no amount of effort can make you better. On the other hand, when you trust you have the ability to improve, you may still doubt yourself, but that doubt does not stop you from taking action and moving forward. When change seems possible, you become unstoppable. You're no longer limited by what you think about yourself or who you're today, you're willing to put in the work to shape your thoughts to align with your goals in the future. Your thoughts, beliefs, and expectations shape your life. They filter the choices you make every day—though you don't realize it. Growth mindset will not rid you of self-doubt, but it will enable you to make the right choices knowing that you have the power to change.

The desire to change with the mindset to sustain those changes over time can turn you into a confident person who isn't limited by feelings of inadequacy and self-doubt, but rather, those feelings signal something important—you're doing valuable work that needs your focus and attention. The imposter feelings that earlier pulled you down will now lift you up by making you more attentive to the process—you will be willing to build new skills, try different strategies, seek varied opinions, ask for help and stick with it long enough to make meaningful progress.

TURN IT INTO A HABIT

Our brain learns from repetition—the more you do something, the stronger it becomes. Charles Duhigg, author of *The Power of Habit* says "Habits emerge because the brain is constantly looking for ways to save effort. Left to its own devices, the brain will try to make almost any routine into a habit, because habits allow our minds to ramp down more often."[3] Habits shape our everyday actions that grow stronger the more we perform them. They shift our minds from proactively making decisions to becoming more and more automatic. Habits are important not only because they conserve less brain power, but also because they create neurological cravings where a certain behavior is rewarded by the release of pleasure chemicals in the brain. This applies to how you deal with your imposter feelings too. When feeling inadequate or not good enough, you can train your brain to repeat actions that will take you closer to your goals.

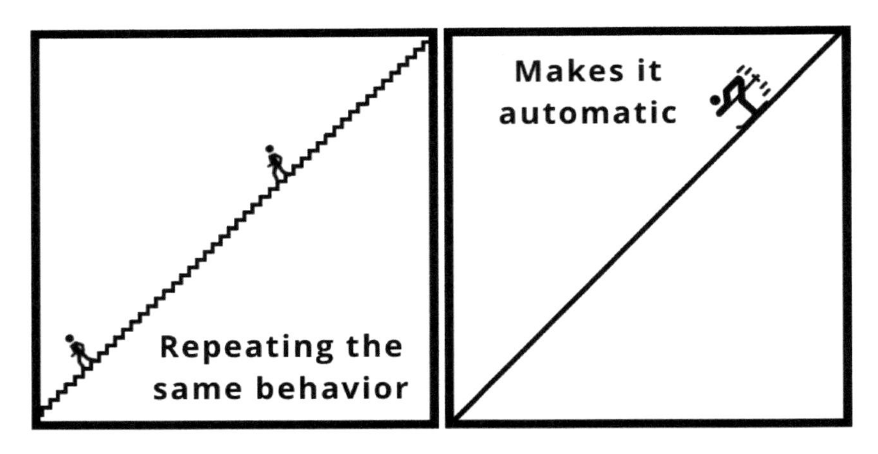

Whenever you feel like an imposter—a feeling that you're not good enough and others will find out soon enough—strengthen the circuits in your brain by taking these actions (a summary of all the strategies in this book):

No.	ACTION ITEM	REMINDER
1	Think about your imposter origin story—where did such thoughts originate?	You didn't have control over your circumstances and conditions that led to feelings of inadequacy and low self-worth, but you now have the power to choose your response.

2	What coping behavior are you tempted to adopt to deal with the feeling that you're not good enough—procrastinator, perfectionist, overworker, people-pleaser, self-diminisher?	Your feelings of inadequacy manifest in your actions as self-sabotage behaviors. These behaviors may look like a shield to protect you from feeling bad about yourself, but all they do is perpetuate your imposter feelings and hold you back.
3	Do not resist your emotions. Invite them in. Acknowledge how you're feeling without judging them or trying to change them.	Ignoring or avoiding your feelings makes them much harder to overcome. Accepting makes you spend less energy in pushing the emotion away and instead pursue the behaviors that are aligned with your goals and values.
4	Give your imposter feelings a voice. Talk to someone trusted, someone who knows and supports you.	Speaking to others reduces their intensity and makes your thoughts less intimidating. It also helps you realize that others feel this way too which makes you more open to talking about it and seeking their opinion.
5	Don't personalize your mistakes and failures. Use	Being occasionally wrong, failing, and not knowing

	them as learning lessons.	something does not make you fake or undeserving. It only makes you human.
6	Set learning goals (focus on self-improvement) as opposed to performance goals (focus on self-validation).	Performance goals turn mistakes into personal failings while learning goals make them part of the learning process.
7	Look to your past achievements as evidence that you're indeed capable and have what it takes. [If you haven't recorded your wins so far, it's time to do the 'Strengths Reflection' exercise from Chapter 11 now]	Your knowledge, skills, and abilities play a much bigger role than luck, hard work, or other factors in your success.
8	Reframe your negative thoughts in a way that empowers you and shifts your negative self-talk from destructive to constructive.	Reframing your thoughts by looking at them through a different lens—one that is more positive—helps you recalibrate your perception of yourself and build the resilience needed to deal with your feelings of unworthiness. Done consistently, this strengthens the new circuits

		in your brain which enables you to repeat this way of thinking more often.
9	Build confidence by taking action, doing the thing—implement tiny steps, measure your results, change and adapt.	Don't wait to build confidence before doing the things you want to do. Confidence comes from getting past your fears by taking action, not from doing nothing.
10	Shift from comparing yourself to others to competing with self—try to become the best version of yourself.	When life is about becoming a better version of yourself, you're no longer concerned with falling short in comparison to others. Rather, what matters is how you're improving, what you're learning, and whether you're getting better each day.
11	Practice self-compassion instead of trying to raise self-esteem.	Stay mindful by keeping a balanced perspective of your emotions, comfort yourself with kindness, and remind yourself that your experience is not unique and everyone struggles with such feelings from time to time.

Repeating the above process every time you feel overwhelmed by imposter thoughts is crucial to a lasting change. You have to feed your brain with these new practices over long periods of time. You have to fire the same circuits, not once or twice, but multiple times to strengthen new ways of thinking and acting. The more you do it, the more they will become part of your being, who you are. They will become second nature. They will turn into a habit. Once a habit, your brain will do all the work behind the scenes for you. It will learn to make decisions that will empower you instead of holding you back.

For example:

- When you achieve something significant, you'll automatically acknowledge your win and celebrate your accomplishment.
- When someone praises you, you'll consider yourself worthy of that praise and say "thank you."
- When you make a mistake or fail at something, you'll use compassion to deal with your feelings and get back on track.
- Receiving criticism won't hurt your self-esteem, you'll consider it as an opportunity to learn and improve.
- A new opportunity or a challenge may lead to feelings of self-doubt, but those feelings will no longer prevent you from reaching for your goals or taking action.
- When building new skills, you won't wait to feel completely confident. You'll gain that confidence through tiny steps.
- To know how you're doing, you'll compare your performance to your past self to determine whether you're improving, staying the same, or getting worse.

Making any change last requires only these three steps—desire to change, mindset to learn, and persistence to turn it into a habit through repetition. As Jacob A. Riis, a social reformer, and photographer describes it "Look at a stone cutter hammering away at his rock, perhaps a hundred times without as much as a crack showing in it. Yet at the hundred-and-first blow it will split in two, and I know it was not the last blow that did it, but all that had gone before." Habits work the same way. Keep repeating the behavior over and over again till it gets you the outcome you desire.

Ending with this beautiful thought from Dale Carnegie:

Inaction breeds doubt
and fear. Action breeds
confidence and courage.
If you want to conquer
fear, do not sit home
and think about it.
Go out and get busy.[4]

Chapter Summary

- Your imposter feelings may never completely go away, but you can always respond to them in a constructive manner. To do this, you have to replace old circuits in your brain that are wired to respond negatively with new behaviors and actions that are aligned with the person you wish to become.
- To make any change last, repetition is the key. The more you do something, the more natural it becomes.
- Once your brain learns the positive actions you take when doubting yourself or feeling inadequate, it will automatically invoke them without your conscious awareness.

- The desire to bring about this positive change in your life is essential, but what's equally important to make this change last is the right mindset. Instead of thinking that your personality and intelligence cannot get better with time and effort, know that you have the power to shape yourself into the person you wish to become.
- Believing that you aren't limited by your current skills and abilities enables you to make the right decisions—decisions that take you closer to your goals and the future you envision.
- Turning these new behaviors into a habit makes them easier to repeat and stick with them long-term.

CONCLUSION

YOUR MIND is a double-edged sword. Its immense power makes it capable of accomplishing both valuable and destructive feats. It works to your advantage when it helps you learn from the past to create your future. Navigating the complexities of life, making decisions, communicating, learning, and improving are part of its bright side. But it also has a dark side that you might fail to realize. When the unpleasant and undesirable part of your mind rears its ugly head, it highlights negative experiences from the past and makes the future appear bleak. It reminds you of your flaws and shortcomings, failures and mistakes, and makes you look smaller compared to others. And it doesn't stop there. Once it's on a roll, it conjures up negative stories making you believe that you're actually inadequate.

Being blindly led by your feelings makes you lose perspective. It gives permission to your mind to hold you hostage by keeping you locked in a place of doubt and fear. You react emotionally, latch onto destructive behaviors and give up opportunities that you are very well suited to perform. Trapped inside this mental prison, you wish to break free. But how?

I hope after reading this book, you now have the answer: your thoughts are just a creation of your mind and not a true measure of your worth. Despite what your mind tells you, you have the power to perceive things differently. No need to run away from these feelings or desperately wait for a day when you no longer feel this way. Your thoughts will never be perfectly aligned with your goals. But that's no longer a reason to worry. Because you can achieve everything you desire and accomplish all your goals by applying the strategies in this book: each step you take will make you stronger, more skilled, more confident and bring you closer to your goals.

Change is possible when you stop believing in your thoughts and start believing in yourself. You don't need a magic wand to transform yourself; a series of tiny steps in everyday moments can turn you into the person you wish to be. Nothing can stop you—not even your imposter feelings—when you know what you want and are willing to put in the work to achieve it. Remember this: the only thing stopping you from bringing about this change in your life is you.

On the days that I struggled to write this book—had trouble structuring my thoughts or was simply distracted by other events in my life—I wanted to be left alone, not bothered. I thought some quiet time would get me back on track. But my mind kept bombarding me with self-defeating thoughts "You're no good!" "No one will read the book if it's not perfect!" "How will you write a book if you can't even put your thoughts together?" It's in those moments that my own strategies came to my rescue. I dealt with my emotions without denying them. I practiced compassion by telling myself that it's ok to have bad days. I reminded myself of my past achievements "I have done this before and I can do it again." It all worked. I got back to writing and built confidence every step of the way. This book is a proof of what these strategies can do once you're willing to make them a part of your life.

Let self-doubt be an ally, an indicator of aspiration. Let it take you closer to your goals and not away from them. All the best!

If I made a mistake somewhere in this book through wrong attribution or failed to give credit where it is due, please email me at vinita@techtello.com so that I can fix the issue and share my gratitude.

Finally, if you believe this book can benefit others around you, make sure to tell them about it. Please share your feedback on the platform where you purchased this book. I'd love to hear about it. Honest reviews help readers find the right book for their needs. Thanks for your support!

ABOUT THE AUTHOR

Vinita Bansal worked in the technology space for many years where she built large engineering teams from the ground up and led products with massive scale impacting millions of customers. Her experience from navigating the challenges and dynamics of a work environment and what it takes to succeed and perform at the highest levels without feeling burnt out, exhausted and overwhelmed inspired her to start *TechTello* where she coaches and mentors people from diverse backgrounds to let go of their limiting beliefs, embrace their unique strengths, and build the skills and support required to grow in their careers so that they feel confident to take on higher level responsibilities within their organizations.

She is inspired by anything that helps shape her thinking, encourages her to doubt her knowledge, and guides her to continue investing in her own learning and growth. She likes to interact with people who defy conventional wisdom and challenge her to have a fresh perspective on life.

You can find more about her work at www.techtello.com or write to her at vinita@techtello.com to connect.

since Notes

INTRODUCTION

1 When feeling is for thinking: Daniel Pink, *The Power of Regret: How Looking Backward Moves Us Forward* (New York : Riverhead Books, 2022)

2 Happiness is the universal: Marshall Goldsmith, "Existential threat is exhausting," *marshallgoldsmith.com*, https://marshallgoldsmith.com/articles/blog-2-existential-regret-is-exhausting/

3 Make money the measure: B.S. Murthy, *Goodreads*, https://www.goodreads.com/quotes/tag/money-minded

4 Meaningful social relationships: Shilo Rea, "Press Release: Social Support: Carnegie Mellon's Brooke Feeney Details How To Thrive Through Close Relationships," *cmu.edu*, September 5, 2014, https://www.cmu.edu/news/stories/archives/2014/september/september5_feeneyrelationshipsupport.html

CHAPTER 1

1 Pauline R. Clance and Suzanne A. Imes in 1978: Pauline R. Clance and Suzanne A. Imes, "The Impostor Phenomenon in High Achieving Women: Dynamics and Therapeutic Intervention," *Psychotherapy: Theory, Research & Practice,* 15 (3), 241–247, doi:10.1037/h0086006

2 It's not who you are: Denis Waitley, *Goodreads*, https://www.goodreads.com/quotes/417268-it-s-not-who-you-are-that-holds-you-back-it-s

3 Achievements don't stamp out: Amy Cuddy, *Presence: Bringing Your Boldest Self to Your Biggest Challenge*s (New York: Little, Brown and Company, 2015), 57

4 Like a boulder chained: "Katya Ederer," *Instagram*, March 1, 2018, https://www.instagram.com/p/BfwcL8Wl3xx/

5 Vulnerability is not weakness: Brené Brown, *Daring Greatly: How the Courage to Be Vulnerable Transforms the Way We Live, Love, Parent, and Lead* (London, England: Portfolio Penguin, 2013), 1-2

CHAPTER 2

1 What is behavioral economics: Dan Ariely, "Pluralistic Ignorance," *Youtube*, Feb 17, 2011, https://www.youtube.com/watch?v=-9wHttUayMo

2 Pluralistic ignorance: "Pluralistic ignorance," *Wikipedia*, October 31, 2021, https://en.wikipedia.org/wiki/Pluralistic_ignorance

3 70% of individuals: Sandeep Ravindran, "Feeling Like A Fraud: The Impostor Phenomenon in Science Writing," *The Open Notebook*, November 15, 2016, https://www.theopennotebook.com/2016/11/15/feeling-like-a-fraud-the-impostor-phenomenon-in-science-writing/

4 Former Olympic pole vaulter: "Personal Story: Managing Imposter Syndrome," *Mentemia*, https://www.mentemia.com/blog/feel-like-an-imposter-youre-not-al one

5 Today I feel like: Christina Pazzanese, "Portman: I, too, battled self-doubt," *The Harvard Gazette*, May 27, 2015, https://news.harvard.edu/gazette/story/2015/05/portman-i-too-batt led-self-doubt/

6 I felt that at any moment: Neil Gaiman, May 12, 2017, https://neil-gaiman.tumblr.com/post/160603396711/hi-i-read-that-youve-dealt-with-with-impostor

CHAPTER 3

1 Hidden and unexpected upsides: Peter Rubinstein, "The hidden upside of imposter syndrome, " *BBC*, March 17, 2021, https://www.bbc.com/worklife/article/20210315-the-hidden-upsid e-of-imposter-syndrome

2 Dunning Kruger effect: The Dunning-Kruger effect occurs when a person's lack of knowledge and skills in a certain area cause them to overestimate their own competence. For more see: "Why can we not perceive our own abilities?," *The Decision Lab*, https://thedecisionlab.com/biases/dunning-kruger-effect/

3 ignorance plus conviction: Tim Urban, "The Thinking Ladder," *Wait But Why*, September 27, 2019, https://waitbutwhy.com/2019/09/thinking-ladder.html

4 having faith in our capability: Adam Grant, *Think Again: The Power of Knowing What You Don't Know* (New York: Viking, 2021), 46-47

5 Let's change thousands: Nicole Laporte, "Inside Bumble CEO Whitney Wolfe Herd's mission to build the female internet," *Fast Company*, September 9, 2019, https://www.fastcompany.com/90396193/inside-bumble-ceo-whitney-wolfe-herds-mission-to-build-the-female-internet

6 It wasn't quite leaping: Robert Iger, The Ride of a Lifetime: Lessons in Creative Leadership from the CEO of the Walt Disney Company (New York: Random House, 2019), 54

CHAPTER 4

1 We pay a heavy price: John W. Gardner, Self-Renewal: The Individual and the Innovative Society (New York : Harper & Row, 1964), 15

2 You gain strength: Eleanor Roosevelt Biography, *Franklin D. Roosevelt Presidential Library and Museum*, https://www.fdrlibrary.org/eleanor-roosevelt

3 relentlessly pushing her comfort zone: Melody Wilding, "Please stop telling me to leave my comfort zone," *The Guardian*, November 17, 2018, https://www.theguardian.com/us-news/2018/nov/16/comfort-zone-mental-health

4 For weeks beforehand: Adam Grant, "How I Overcame the Fear of Public Speaking," *LinkedIn*, September 18, 2014, https://www.linkedin.com/pulse/20140918134337-69244073-overcoming-the-fear-of-public-speaking/

5 three zones when it comes to comfort: Anisa Purbasari Horton, "This is when stepping outside your comfort zone is a bad idea, " *Fast Company*, April 29, 2019, https://www.fastcompany.com/90336528/when-you-shouldnt-step-outside-your-comfort-zone

6 Enjoyment appears at the boundary: Mihaly Csikszentmihalyi, *Flow: The Psychology of Happiness* (London: Ebury Publishing, 2013), 52

7 **Goldilocks rule:** "Goldilocks principle," *Wikipedia*, February 3, 2021, https://en.wikipedia.org/wiki/Goldilocks_principle

CHAPTER 5

1 take into account: Sanne Feenstra, Christopher T. Begeny, Michelle K. Ryan, Floor A. Rink, Janka I. Stoker, Jennifer Jordan, "Contextualizing the Impostor Syndrome," *Frontiers in Psychology*, 11 (2020), doi: 10.3389/fpsyg.2020.575024

2 I never asked a question: Katherine M. Caflisch, "Imposter Syndrome: The Truth About Feeling Like a Fake," *American Society for Microbiology*, August 14, 2020, https://asm.org/Articles/2020/August/Imposter-Syndrome-The-Truth-About-Feeling-Like-a-F

3 She left Egypt: "We need to humanise technology before it dehumanises us," *Campaign UK*, July 07, 2020, https://www.campaignlive.co.uk/article/we-need-humanise-technology-dehumanises-us/1688687

4 I was a woman: Sheryl Nance-Nash, "Why imposter syndrome hits women and women of colour harder," *BBC*, July 28, 2020, https://www.bbc.com/worklife/article/20200724-why-imposter-syndrome-hits-women-and-women-of-colour-harder

5 family history with anxiety: Loretta Mcgregor & Damon E. Gee & K. Elizabeth Posey, "I feel like a fraud and it depresses me: The relation between the imposter phenomenon and depression," *Social Behavior and Personality: An international journal*, 36(2008), 43-48, doi: 10.2224/sbp.2008.36.1.43

6 high academic achievements: Julie E. King & Eileen L. Cooley, "Achievement orientation and the impostor phenomenon among college students," *Contemporary Educational Psychology*, 20(1995), 304–312, doi: 10.1006/ceps.1995.1019

7 I sort of internalized: Lulu Garcia-Navarro, "Imposter Syndrome, Or Something Else? Historian Talks Discriminatory Gaslighting," *npr.org*, May 9, 2021, https://www.npr.org/2021/05/09/995172973/imposter-syndrome-or-something-else-historian-talks-discriminatory-gaslighting

8 I thought they only hired me: Maureen Zappala, "About Maureen," *maureenz*, https://maureenz.com/about/

9 women and people from ethnic minorities: John FDovidio, NancyEvans, Richard BTyler, "Racial stereotypes: the contents of their cognitive representations," *Journal of Experimental Social Psychology*, 22 (1986), 22–37, doi: 10.1016/0022-1031(86)90039-9; Naomi Ellemers, "Gender stereotypes," *Annual Review of Psychology*, 69 (2018), 275–298, doi: 10.1146/annurev-psych-122216-011719; Alice H Eagly, Steven J. Karau, "Role congruity theory of prejudice toward female leaders," *Psychological review*, 109 (2002), 573-98, doi: 10.1037//0033-295X.109.3.573; Christine Reyna, "Lazy, Dumb, or Industrious: When Stereotypes Convey Attribution Information in the Classroom," *Educational Psychology Review*, 12 (2000), 85–110, doi: 10.1023/A:1009037101170

10 Expectations also shape stereotypes: Dan Ariely, *Predictably Irrational: The Hidden Forces That Shape Our Decision*s (New York :HarperCollins, 2008), 168-169

11 studies reveal biases in the workplace: Kim Parker & Cary Funk, "Gender discrimination comes in many forms for today's working women," *Pew Research Center*, December 14, 2017, https://www.pewresearch.org/fact-tank/2017/12/14/gender-discrimination-comes-in-many-forms-for-todays-working-women/

12 under-represented in surgery: Sanne Feenstra, Christopher T. Begeny, Michelle K. Ryan, Floor A. Rink, Janka I. Stoker, Jennifer Jordan, "Contextualizing the Impostor Syndrome," *Frontiers in Psychology*, 11 (2020), doi: 10.3389/fpsyg.2020.575024

13 Discover your origin story: Trish Taylor, *Yes! You Are Good Enough: End Imposter Syndrome, Overthinking and Perfectionism and Do What YOU Wan*t (Taylored NLP 2020), 25

CHAPTER 6

1 research has shown that: Debbara Dingman, "The impostor phenomenon and social mobility: You can't go home again," *Dissertation Abstracts International*, 49 (1988); Joe Langford & Pauline Rose Clance, "The impostor phenomenon: recent research findings regarding dynamics, personality and family patterns and their implications for treatment," *Psychotherapy: Theory, Research, Practice, Training*, 30 (1993): 495–501, doi:10.1037/0033-3204.30.3.495

2 one study that explored: Rebecca Badawy & Brooke Gazdag & Jeffrey Bentley & Robyn Brouer, "Are all impostors created equal? Exploring gender differences in the impostor phenomenon-performance link," *Personality and Individual Differences*, 131 (2018), 156-163, doi: 10.1016/j.paid.2018.04.044

3 Don't fake it 'til you make it: Amy Cuddy, "Amy Cuddy TED Talk - Fake it Till You Make it," *Youtube*, July 8, 2016, https://www.youtube.com/watch?v=RVmMeMcGc0Y

4 I postured and pretended: Laura Huang, "Why 'Fake It Till You Make It' Is Terrible Advice," *time,* February 5, 2020, https://time.com/5777479/fake-it-till-make-it-advice/

5 It literally means you can't do it: Vivian Manning-Schaffel, "Fake It Till You Make It: Good Advice or a Setup for Failure?," *Shondaland*, February 18, 2022, https://www.shondaland.com/live/money/a39125630/fake-it-till-you-make-it-good-advice-or-a-setup-for-failure/

6 CEO of Social Entrepreneurs: Darren Ryan, "Embracing Imposter Syndrome," *LinkedIn*, December 6, 2019, https://www.linkedin.com/pulse/embracing-imposter-syndrome-darren-ryan/

7 Mental health issues: Jasmine Vergauwe & Bart Wille & Marjolein Feys & Filip De Fruyt & Frederik Anseel, "Fear of Being Exposed: The Trait-Relatedness of the Impostor Phenomenon and its Relevance in the Work Context," *Journal of Business and Psychology*, 30 (2015), doi: 10.1007/s10869-014-9382-5

8 Harmful coping strategies: Holly Hutchins & Hilary Rainbolt, "What triggers imposter phenomenon among academic faculty? A critical incident study exploring antecedents, coping, and development opportunities," *Human Resource Development International*, 20 (2016), 1-21, doi: 10.1080/13678868.2016.1248205

9 intentionally pass up opportunities: Shaun Cowman & Joseph Ferrari, "Am I for real? Predicting impostor tendencies from self-handicapping and affective components," *Social Behavior and Personality: an international journal*, 30 (2002), 119-125, doi: 10.2224/sbp.2002.30.2.119

CHAPTER 7

1 We can become obsessed: Emma Gannon, "The Truth About Self-Sabotage And Why We're Afraid Of Success," *Elle*, September 18, 2019, https://www.elle.com/uk/life-and-culture/culture/a29101686/self-sabotage-happiness/

2 The source of self-sabotage: Judy Ho, "Why We Self-Sabotage," *Psychology Today*, November 2, 2019, https://www.psychologytoday.com/ca/blog/unlock-your-true-motivation/201911/why-we-self-sabotage

3 Handing things in late: Georgina Lawton, "I'm a self-saboteur—why do I fear success more than failure?," *The Guardian*, December 2, 2017, https://www.theguardian.com/lifeandstyle/2017/dec/02/im-a-self-saboteur-why-do-i-fear-success-more-than-failure

4 If I didn't say yes to everything: Alan Light, "How Brandi Carlile Overcame Impostor Syndrome," *Wall Street Journal*, August 17, 2021, https://www.wsj.com/articles/brandi-carlile-interview-impostor-syndrome-11629203534

5 Perfectionism has nothing to do: Julia Cameron, *The Artist's Way: A Spiritual Path to Higher Creativity* (New York : Jeremy P. Tarcher/Putnam, 2002), 228-230

6 the 20-ton shield: Lisa Capretto, "Overcoming Perfectionism: Brené Brown Talks Perfection And Authenticity With Oprah," *HuffPost*, June 29, 2013, https://www.huffpost.com/entry/brene-brown-daring-greatly-perfectionism-oprah_n_3468501

7 We think, mistakenly: Arianna Huffington, *Thrive: The Third Metric to Redefining Success and Creating a Life of Well-Being, Wisdom, and Wonder* (New York : Random House, 2014), 51

8 being nice is about being liked: Aziz Gazipura, *Not Nice: Stop People Pleasing, Staying Silent, & Feeling Guilty... And Start Speaking Up, Saying No, Asking Boldly, And Unapologetically Being Yourself* (Portland, OR : B.C. Allen Publishing & Tonic Books, 2017), 12

CHAPTER 8

1 The company claimed to revolutionize: Zaw Thiha Tun, "Theranos: A Fallen Unicorn," *Investopedia*, January 4, 2022, https://www.investopedia.com/articles/investing/020116/theranos-fallen-unicorn.asp; "Theranos," *Wikipedia*, March 7, 2022, https://en.wikipedia.org/wiki/Theranos

2 Newmann had voted: Matthew Zeitlin, "Why WeWork went wrong," *The Guardian*, December 20, 2019, https://www.theguardian.com/business/2019/dec/20/why-wework-went-wrong; "WeWork," *Wikipedia*, March 8, 2022, https://en.wikipedia.org/wiki/WeWork

3 According to the survey: Roger Jones, "What CEOs Are Afraid Of," *Harvard Business Review*, February 24, 2015, https://hbr.org/2015/02/what-ceos-are-afraid-of

4 Why would people invest themselves: Fred Johnson, "I am Enough," *Youtube*, November 14, 2018, https://www.youtube.com/watch?v=bfJzsReaR5E

CHAPTER 9

1 Attempts at avoiding negative emotions: Noam Shpancer, "Emotional Acceptance: Why Feeling Bad is Good," *Psychology Today*, September 8, 2010, https://www.psychologytoday.com/us/blog/insight-therapy/201009/emotional-acceptance-why-feeling-bad-is-good

2 Buddha and demon Mara: Tara Brach, *Radical Acceptance: Awakening the Love That Heals Fear and Shame* (New York : Bantam Books, 2004), 66-67

3 The opposite of recognizing: Brené Brown, Rising Strong: How the Ability to Reset Transforms the Way We Live, Love, Parent, and Lead (New York : Spiegel & Grau), 51

4 airing imposter struggles with peers: Chris Palmer, "How to overcome impostor phenomenon," *American Psychological Association*, June 1, 2021, https://www.apa.org/monitor/2021/06/cover-impostor-phenomenon

5 it can be helpful to connect: Chris Palmer, "How to overcome impostor phenomenon," *American Psychological Association*, June 1, 2021, https://www.apa.org/monitor/2021/06/cover-impostor-phenomenon

6 From starting out as an associate: Alvin Tan, "How imposter syndrome can help," *LinkedIn*, https://www.linkedin.com/posts/alvinshtan_impostersyndrome-ourimposterstories-activity-6817844542822318080-4aWM/

7 This exercise is taken: Tara Brach, *Radical Acceptance: Awakening the Love That Heals Fear and Shame* (New York : Bantam Books, 2004), 75-76

CHAPTER 10

1 It's not what happens to you: Epictetus, *goodreads.com*, https://www.goodreads.com/quotes/239288-it-s-not-what-happens-to-you-but-how-you-react

2 Failure doesn't make you a fraud: Jessica Bennett, "How to Overcome Impostor Syndrome," *The New York Times*, https://www.nytimes.com/guides/working-womans-handbook/over come-impostor-syndrome

3 CV of failures: Josh Hrala, "This Princeton Professor's CV of Failures Is Something We Should All Learn From," *Science Alert*, December 25, 2017, https://www.sciencealert.com/why-creating-a-cv-of-failures-is-good-Princeton-professor-viral; "CV of failures: Princeton professor publishes résumé of his career lows," *The Guardian*, April 30, 2016, https://www.theguardian.com/education/2016/apr/30/cv-of-failure s-princeton-professor-publishes-resume-of-his-career-lows

4 In one experiment: Bec Crew, "Science Students Get Better Grades When They Know Einstein And Marie Curie Also Struggled," *Science Alert*, February 26, 2016, https://www.sciencealert.com/science-students-do-better-when-they -know-einstein-and-curie-also-struggled

5 types of goals you set: Heidi Grant, *Succeed: How We Can Reach Our Goals* (New York, N.Y. : Hudson Street Press, 2011), 59

6 main differences between two types of goals: Summarized key differences using this book: Heidi Grant, *Succeed: How We Can Reach Our Goals* (New York, N.Y. : Hudson Street Press, 2011), 57-70

7 with a performance mindset: Andy Molinsky, "Everyone Suffers from Impostor Syndrome — Here's How to Handle It," *Harvard Business Review*, July 7, 2016, https://hbr.org/2016/07/everyone-suffers-from-imposter-syndrome-heres-how-to-handle-it

8 See the world as: Jenny Darmody, "Imposter syndrome: How to deal with feeling like a failure at work," *Silicon Republic*, August 28, 2017, https://www.siliconrepublic.com/advice/imposter-syndrome-failure-work-gerry-hussey

CHAPTER 11

1 Her imposter syndrome kicked in: Luvvie Ajayi Jones, "About My TED Talk That Almost Didn't Happen and Now Has 2 Million Views," *awesomelyluvvie*, April 9, 2018, https://awesomelyluvvie.com/2018/04/about-my-ted-talk-2-million-views.html

2 Imposter syndrome absolutely lies to us: Padma Warrior, "The Power of Impostor Syndrome," *fable.co*, https://fable.co/events/the-power-of-impostor-syndrome

3 Imposter syndrome is a paradox: Adam Grant, *Twitter*, November 14, 2021, https://twitter.com/adammgrant/status/1459894544884015113

4 Our job in this lifetime: Steven Pressfield, *The War of Art: Break Through the Blocks and Win Your Inner Creative Battles* (New York, NY : Black Irish Entertainment, LLC, 2012), 145

CHAPTER 12

1 My son, the battle: "Tow Wolves," *Wikipedia*, March 23, 2022, https://en.wikipedia.org/wiki/Two_Wolves

2 Neurons that fire together: "What does "neurons that fire together wire together" mean?," *Supercamp*, https://www.supercamp.com/what-does-neurons-that-fire-together-wire-together-mean/

3 What you do now: Jeffrey Schwartz, *You Are Not Your Brain: The 4-Step Solution for Changing Bad Habits, Ending Unhealthy Thinking, and Taking Control of Your Life* (New York: Avery, 2011), 31

4 It's one of those two: Clay Skipper, "Why Mindfulness is the Next Frontier in Sports Performance," *GQ*, February 26, 2020, https://www.gq.com/story/michael-gervais-sports-psychology-interview

5 Once he was pulled out: "Feel like a fraud? You're not alone. Top execs share their stories of imposter syndrome and how they overcame it," *University of Queensland*, https://business.uq.edu.au/momentum/imposter-syndrome

6 She doubted herself: Yunita Ong, "How imposter syndrome can help," *LinkedIn*, June 2021, https://www.linkedin.com/posts/yunitaong_ourimposterstories-personaldevelopment-careers-activity-6817993050976002048-P1Ip/

7 Mindfulness guides us: Susan David, *Emotional Agility* (New York : Avery an imprint of Penguin Random House, 2016), 81

8 This technique introduced by psychologist: Dalai Lama Center for Peace and Education, "Dan Siegel: Name it to Tame it," *Youtube*, December 8, 2014, https://www.youtube.com/watch?v=ZcDLzppD4Jc

9 His research has shown that: Matthew Lieberman, Tristen Inagaki, Golnaz Tabibnia & Molly Crockett, "Subjective responses to emotional stimuli during labeling, reappraisal, and distraction," *Emotion*, 11 (2011), 468-480, doi: 10.1037/a0023503; Matthew Lieberman & Naomi Eisenberger & Molly Crockett & Sabrina Tom & Jennifer Pfeifer & Baldwin Way, "Putting Feelings Into Words," *Psychological science*, 18 (2007), 421-8, doi: 10.1111/j.1467-9280.2007.01916.x.

10 The secret of getting ahead: Mark Twain, *goodreads.com*, https://www.goodreads.com/quotes/219455-the-secret-of-getting-ahead-is-getting-started-the-secret

11 Between stimulus and response: Victor E. Frankl, *goodreads.com*, https://www.goodreads.com/quotes/8144491-between-stimulus-and-response-there-is-a-space-in-that

CHAPTER 13

1 Success correlates more closely: Katty Kay & Claire Shimpan, *The Confidence Code: The Science and Art of Self-Assurance---What Women Should Know* (New York, NY : HarperBusiness, an imprint of HarperCollinsPublishers, 2014), 11

2 A sample of 48 people: Barry R. Schlenker & Mark R. Leary, "Audiences' reactions to self-enhancing, self-denigrating, and accurate self-presentations," *Journal of Experimental Social Psychology*, 18 (1982), 89-104, doi: 10.1016/0022-1031(82)90083-x

3 the ability or the belief: Dr. Ivan Joseph, "The skill of self confidence," *youtube.com*, Jan 13, 2012, https://www.youtube.com/watch?v=w-HYZv6HzAs

4 Derived from a latin word: "Confidence," *Wikipedia.com*, March 16, 2022, https://en.wikipedia.org/wiki/Confidence

5 I have to feel confident: Russ Harris, *The Confidence Gap: A Guide to Overcoming Fear and Self-Doubt* (London : Robinson, 2011), 21

6 The actions of confidence: Russ Harris, *The Confidence Gap: A Guide to Overcoming Fear and Self-Doubt* (London : Robinson, 2011), 22

7 own struggles with confidence: Russ Harris, *The Confidence Gap: A Guide to Overcoming Fear and Self-Doubt* (London : Robinson, 2011), 11-12

8 Small wins are exactly: Charles Duhigg, *The Power of Habit: Why We Do What We Do in Life and Business* (New York : Random House, 2012), 111-112

9 by simply writing down a plan: Sarah Milne, Sheina Orbell & Paschal Sheeran, "Combining motivational and volitional interventions to promote exercise participation: Protection motivation theory and implementation intentions," *British journal of health psychology*, 7 (2002), 163-84, doi: 10.1348/135910702169420

10 What's measured improves: Peter Drucker, *goodreads.com*, https://www.goodreads.com/quotes/172730-what-s-measured-impr oves

11 Feeling out of place: P. Bodi, *Instagram.com*, October 4, 2019, https://www.instagram.com/p/B3M8vqPFjVB/

CHAPTER 14

1 social comparison theory: Leon Festinger, "A theory of social comparison processes," Human Relations, 7 (1954), 117–140, doi: 10.1177/001872675400700202

2 we make downward comparisons: Juliana Breines, "The Perils of Comparing Ourselves to Others," *Psychology Today*, July 31, 2016, https://www.psychologytoday.com/intl/blog/in-love-and-war/2016 07/the-perils-comparing-ourselves-others

3 positive or negative quality: Richard Smith, "Assimilative and Contrastive Emotional Reactions to Upward and Downward Social Comparison," *Journal of Experimental Social Psychology*, 41 (2000), doi: 10.1007/978-1-4615-4237-7_10

4 four possible types: Bram Buunk & Hans Kuyper & Yvonne Zee, "Affective Response to Social Comparison in the Classroom," *Basic and Applied Social Psychology - BASIC APPL SOC PSYCHOL*, 27 (2005), 229-237, doi: 10.1207/s15324834basp2703_4; Richard Smith, "Assimilative and Contrastive Emotional Reactions to Upward and Downward Social Comparison," *Journal of Experimental Social Psychology*, 41 (2000), doi: 10.1007/978-1-4615-4237-7_10; B. P. Buunk, & J. F. Ybema, "Social comparisons and occupational stress: The identification-contrast model. In B. P. Buunk & F. X. Gibbons (Eds.)," *Health, coping, and well-being: Perspectives from social comparison theory*, 1997, 359–388, Lawrence Erlbaum Associates Publishers

5 your self-evaluation: Marie-Hélène Chayer & Thérèse Bouffard, "Relations between impostor feelings and upward and downward identification and contrast among 10- To 12-year-old students," *European Journal of Psychology of Education*, 25 (2010), 125-140, doi: 10.1007/s10212-009-0004-y

6 One of the biggest: Oliver Burkeman, "Everyone is totally just winging it, all the time," *The Guardian*, May 21, 2014, https://www.theguardian.com/news/oliver-burkeman-s-blog/2014/may/21/everyone-is-totally-just-winging-it

7 inner scorecard: Tom Popomaronis, "Billionaire Warren Buffett has a 'simple' test for making tough decisions—here's how it works," *cnbc.com*, May 11, 2019, https://www.cnbc.com/2019/05/10/billionaire-warren-buffett-use-this-simple-test-when-making-tough-decisions.html

8 Each of you run: Brett Ledbetter, "How to stop comparing and start competing," *youtube.com*, January 26, 2017, https://www.youtube.com/watch?v=bU09Y9sC7JY

9 self-esteem does not lead: Roy Baumeister & Jennifer Campbell & Joachim Krueger & Kathleen Vohs, "Does High Self-Esteem Cause Better Performance, Interpersonal Success, Happiness, or Healthier Lifestyles?," *Psychological Science in the Public Interest*, 4 (2003), 1-44, doi: 10.1111/1529-1006.01431

10 Instead of mercilessly judging: Dr. Kristin Neff, *self-compassion.org*, https://self-compassion.org/the-three-elements-of-self-compassion-2/

11 emotional resilience: Ricks Warren & Elke Smeets & Kristin Neff, "Self-criticism and self-compassion: Risk and resilience: Being compassionate to oneself is associated with emotional resilience and psychological well-being," *self-compassion.org*, December 2016, https://self-compassion.org/wp-content/uploads/2016/12/Self-Criticism.pdf

12 avoidance tendencies: Kristin Neff, Ya-Ping Hsieh & Kullaya Pisitsungkagarn, "Self-compassion, Achievement Goals, and Coping with Academic Failure," *Self and Identity*, 4 (2005), 263-287, doi: 10.1080/13576500444000317

13 People who are self-compassionate: Kristin Neff & Stephanie Rude & Kristin Kirkpatrick, "An examination of self-compassion in relation to positive psychological functioning and personality traits," *Journal of Research in Personality*, 41 (2007), 908-916, doi: 10.1016/j.jrp.2006.08.002

14 three essential components: Kristin Neff, *Self Compassion* (London: Hodder and Stoughton, 2011), 41

15 Instead of seeing ourselves: Kristin Neff, *Self Compassion* (London: Hodder and Stoughton, 2011), 49

16 When we're in touch: Kristin Neff, *Self Compassion* (London: Hodder and Stoughton, 2011), 62

17 Our sense of self: Kristin Neff, *Self Compassion* (London: Hodder and Stoughton, 2011), 82-83

18 Mindfulness brings us back: Kristin Neff, *Self Compassion* (London: Hodder and Stoughton, 2011), 85

19 This exercise is developed: Kristin Neff, *self-compassion.org*, June 2015, https://self-compassion.org/wp-content/uploads/2015/06/Self_Compassion_Scale_for_researchers.pdf

20 People are like: "Elisabeth Kübler-Ross," *en.wikiquote.org*, February 9, 2022, https://en.wikiquote.org/wiki/Elisabeth_K%C3%BCbler-Ross

CHAPTER 15

1 A person with a fixed mindset: Vinita Bansal, *Upgrade Your Mindset* (Self Published, 2021), 14-17

2 Research from Carol Dweck: Carol Dweck, Carol. (2008) "Can Personality Be Changed? The Role of Beliefs in Personality and Change," *Current Directions in Psychological Science - CURR DIRECTIONS PSYCHOL SCI*, 17 (2008), doi: 10.1111/j.1467-8721.2008.00612.x; Roberts BW, Luo J, Briley DA, Chow PI, Su R, Hill PL, "A systematic review of personality trait change through intervention," *Psychol Bull*, 143(2017), 117-141, doi: 10.1037/bul0000088

3 Habits emerge: Charles Duhigg, *The Power of Habit: Why We Do What We Do in Life and Business* (New York : Random House, 2012), 17

4 Inaction breeds doubt: Dale Carnegie, *goodreads.com*, https://www.goodreads.com/quotes/1140103-inaction-breeds-doub t-and-fear-action-breeds-confidence-and-courage

To request permissions, contact the publisher at vinita@techtello.com.

First Edition

www.techtello.com

Printed in France by Amazon
Brétigny-sur-Orge, FR